Kim Boekman
2003

FLAMEWORKING

creating glass
beads, sculptures &
functional objects

FLAMEWORKING

Elizabeth Ryland Mears

creating glass beads, sculptures & functional objects

LARK BOOKS

A Division of Sterling Publishing Co., Inc.
New York

Editor: Katherine Duncan Aimone
Art Director: Tom Metcalf
Photographer: Keith Wright (www.keithwright.com)
Cover Designer: Barbara Zaretsky
Art Assistant: Shannon Yokeley
Editorial Assistance: Rain Newcomb, Veronika Alice Gunter, Delores Gosnell

10 9 8 7 6 5 4 3 2 1

First Edition

Published by Lark Books, a division of
Sterling Publishing Co., Inc.
387 Park Avenue South, New York, N.Y. 10016

© 2003, Elizabeth Ryland Mears

Distributed in Canada by Sterling Publishing,
c/o Canadian Manda Group, One Atlantic Ave., Suite 105
Toronto, Ontario, Canada M6K 3E7

Distributed in the U.K. by Guild of Master Craftsman Publications Ltd., Castle Place, 166 High Street, Lewes, East Sussex,
England BN7 1XU Tel: (+ 44) 1273 477374, Fax: (+ 44) 1273 478606, Email: pubs@thegmcgroup.com,
Web: www.gmcpublications.com

Distributed in Australia by Capricorn Link (Australia) Pty Ltd.,
P.O. Box 704, Windsor, NSW 2756 Australia

If you have questions or comments about this book, please contact:
Lark Books
67 Broadway
Asheville, NC 28801
(828) 253-0467
Manufactured in China

ISBN 1-57990-298-7

contents

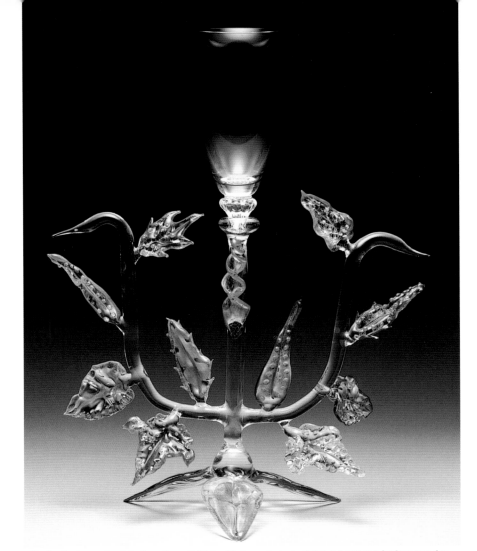

Elizabeth Mears, *Leaf Series: Clear Goblet with Aqua Leaves.* 1993. 14 x 9 x 4 inches (35.6 x 22.9 x 10.2 cm). Flameworked borosilicate glass, assembled. Photo by John Russell

introduction

Welcome! You're entering the wonderful world of flameworking. There is something very special about taking a rod of cold glass, heating it in the flame of a torch, manipulating it a bit, and almost instantaneously creating an object that didn't previously exist. Working at the flame reaches down into the primitive depths of everyone who experiences it.

The exercises in this book are similar to the ones that I use in beginning flameworking workshops. They are followed by projects that incorporate what you've learned. Explicit and detailed how-to photographs that demonstrate working with molten glass will assist you as you work. If you follow them in the order given, and allow yourself a bit of time to

master each, you'll be surprised at how quickly you'll become comfortable with the glass and your torch.

In this book, I'll take you step-by-step through acquiring the equipment you need, setting up your studio and workbench, and working with the glass. The studio setup for flameworking is relatively simple and doesn't require a lot of space—making flameworking more accessible than most other methods of manipulating hot glass.

As a beginning flameworker, you must take specific safety measures when working in a studio with gases and a hot torch. Safety precautions are given throughout the book. Nevertheless, you are ultimately responsible for your own health and studio safety. Every studio setup is individual, so you must be aware of the building codes and regulations in your area, as well as insurance requirements that apply.

You'll begin by making very simple shapes before progressing to more complicated ones. To become proficient at this art, you'll spend hours of time working at the torch as I did, but you'll have a lot of fun while you're learning.

Learning to use your torch is an essential in flameworking. There will be times when you'll need a small, pinpoint flame and other times when you'll need a large, hot flame. You'll constantly turn your torch up and down to adjust the amount of oxygen you use. At first this may seem difficult

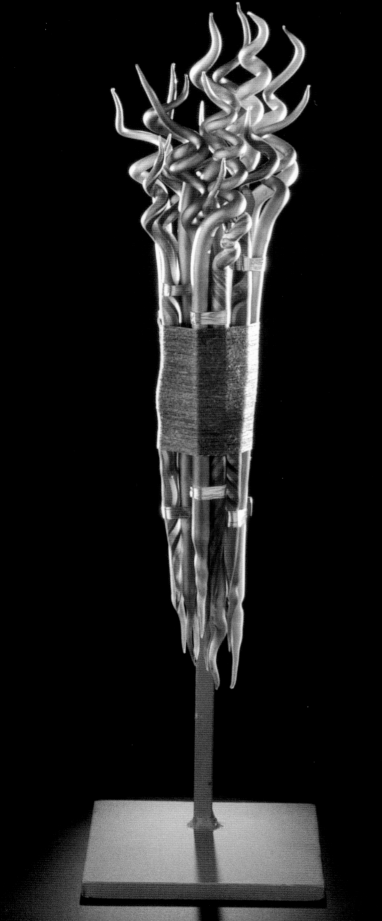

and require a lot of your attention, but as you work, this process becomes automatic.

After you've tried making the different shapes and objects in the beginning exercises, pick a shape and make it over and over using both clear and colored glass. This process will allow you to learn many of the secrets that glass has to share and become more comfortable with them. You'll also become familiar with the characteristics of different colors.

When I began learning flameworking, I limited myself to making very simple discs that looked like lollipops. I made dozens and dozens of them in various sizes and colors. Consequently, I learned lots of valuable lessons, including how to use my torch to get the exact amount of heat needed to shape an object and how to place it precisely for the effect that I wanted to create.

Some of you may come to flameworking hoping that you'll be able to translate shapes and designs that you've used in other media into glass. As you learn from the exercises and projects in this book, you'll develop skills that will eventually enable you to adapt the glass as you wish. Through a lot of practice and some experimentation, you'll formulate ways to use simple methods of working with glass to express your own artistic vision.

Elizabeth Mears, *Large Bundle of Curly Twigs*. 2001. 19 x 7 x 5 inches (48.3 x 17.8 x 12.7 cm). Flameworked borosilicate glass, sandblasted; lusters, copper, waxed linen, steel. Photo by Tommy Elder

glass basics

Glass is a wonderful, amorphous material unlike any other on the face of the earth. It exists in natural forms such as *obsidian*, a dark or black volcanic glass, and *fulgurite*, a glassy, tube-shaped substance that is formed when lightning strikes sand. There are many stories of how humans first began to make glass, but no clear evidence exists as to when glass was first manufactured and used. We do know that the Egyptians were using glass almost 3600 years ago.

There are two types of glass used in flameworking—*"soft" glass* and *"hard" glass*—references that have nothing to do with how easily they break. For all of the exercises in this book, we'll be using hard glass. Glass is made of sand and some chemical flux that causes the sand to fuse together under certain conditions and temperatures. Soft glass uses soda-lime or lead as its flux and melts at lower temperatures, while hard glass (more commonly known as *borosilicate*) uses borax and melts at high temperatures. As a result of these distinctions, the two kinds of glass have very different working characteristics that are suited for some objects and not others.

The expansion and contraction of glass under various conditions of heat influence its workability. Related to this factor and described below are explanations of *coefficient of expansion*, *compatibility*, and *annealing*.

coefficient of expansion

The science of glass is a fascinating subject that is explained in this section in useful and basic terms. Everything on earth, with the exception of a few materials such as water, will expand when heated and contract when cooled. Water is an exception to this physical rule of materials; it contracts to its maximum density at 4°C (39.2 F) before it begins to expand again as it freezes to form ice. The amount of expansion and contraction—an amount so small that it is usually undetectable in our daily lives—can be measured very precisely within a given range of temperature. Some materials move more than others. For instance, metals expand and contract perceptibly as temperatures change, and this is why thermostats contain a long coil of metal for detecting temperature fluctuations. Both alcohol and mercury thermometers also depend on thermal expansion to indicate temperature.

The degree to which a material expands and contracts at a fixed range of temperature is known as its coefficient of expansion (COE). Although it is actually a number multiplied by ten to some factor, it is given as a whole number for our purposes. The COE for soft glasses ranges from 89 to about 109, while the range for borosilicate glass is 32 to 33. The difference in these numbers tells us that soft glass expands and contracts considerably more than hard glass when it is heated or cooled. Therefore, the COE greatly affects how the glass is worked, as well as the size of the pieces that can be made. Some of the differences between soft and borosilicate glass are noted below. There are positive and negative aspects about each type of glass.

◆ Borosilicate glass can usually be plunged directly into the flame without having to warm it, while soft glass must be warmed beforehand to prevent it from exploding.

◆ Molten soft glass has a much longer working time when it is taken out of the flame than borosilicate glass.

◆ Depending on their thickness, many objects made of borosilicate glass don't need to be annealed right away, while soft glass needs to be annealed immediately. (See section below for an explanation of annealing.)

◆ Borosilicate glass can be worked into rather sizable objects, while soft glass usually can't be worked into large objects without considerable technical skill and equipment.

◆ *Creases* (or sharp indentations in the surface of the glass) don't seem to affect the structure of objects made of soft glass, while creases in borosilicate glass are almost always a crack waiting to happen. (See page 25 for more information about creases.)

◆ The working temperature for soft glass is lower than that of borosilicate glass, resulting in a much greater range of colors in soft glass. Nevertheless, there is a wide range of colors available in borosilicate today.

compatibility

Compatibility or "fit" of one glass with another determines whether two glasses can be effectively combined. For two glasses to be compatible, the COE can't differ by more than a couple of numbers. For this reason, soft glass can't be combined with borosilicate in the molten state because it would shrink more, causing the combined piece to crack at the

interface between the two types. Compatibility is also a factor if you're joining glass with other materials, such as metal.

If you know the COEs of the glasses that you plan to combine, you can determine their compatibility. For learning through the exercises and projects in this book, you should combine only clear or colored borosilicate. If you have two types of glass with unknown COEs, you can test their compatibility (see page 38 for an explanation of this test).

annealing

To avoid stress and potential cracking, all glass must be annealed (heated to a certain temperature) after it has been in the flame. Soft glass should be annealed almost immediately after it has been removed from the flame. Borosilicate glass can usually be allowed to cool to room temperature without annealing it right away.

You can anneal glass in the torch's flame or in an annealing kiln. Flame annealing works well for small or thin-walled blown objects, but is impractical for large or thick pieces. For these objects, you'll need an annealing kiln.

Why is annealing so important? The answer lies in the molecular structure of glass, which is composed of separate molecules of the same material packed together in a given volume. When heat is applied, it is absorbed by the molecules, and they become agitated and eventually begin to move around. The more heat is applied, the more the molecules move. If enough heat is applied, the glass will become molten.

As a result of the heat, the molecules reorient their positions in relationship to one another, especially if work is done to the glass such as stretching, pulling, or twisting. As the glass cools, the molecules on the outside cool and contract before the ones on the inside, causing stress between them.

You can actually see this stress if you look at the glass through a *polariscope*—an instrument made up of two polarized lenses. When seen through this instrument, the stress is really quite beautiful, resembling the colors of an oil slick on water.

If the stress isn't removed from the glass, it may crack (see pages 26 and 27 for more information about cracks). In the case of borosilicate, this can happen quickly or much later after you've finished working on a piece. Unless you're making practice pieces (as you will in the exercises), don't skip the final step of annealing the glass. You'll have wasted a lot of your time if the piece falls apart later.

Before you anneal glass, take it up to the melting temperature and complete whatever work that's to be done. As it cools, the glass will be full of stress at this

point. When annealed, it is raised to the temperature at which the molecules barely begin to move in relationship to one other. (The annealing temperature is not high enough for you to be able to perceive movement, but the molecules are quivering in there.) This temperature must be retained long enough to allow all of the molecules to settle into position and eliminate the stress.

(When I teach my workshops, I use the following graphic example to help explain annealing. Let's compare the glass molecules to a group of puppies that are nursing. They're all lined up, plugged in, and as happy as can be. If another one comes along and wants to plug in too, that means that all the others have to shuffle around to make room for the new one. This is similar to what happens when glass is annealed! All of the molecules have to shuffle around to new positions during annealing.)

Glass can't be over-annealed. In fact, you can hold it at the annealing temperature for as long as you want. You'll be able to determine how much time is needed for annealing by trial and error. You can also check the completed objects by looking at them through a polariscope.

To flame-anneal a smaller piece made from borosilicate, begin with a large, yellow propane flame at the end of your torch (photo 1). (See pages 19 and 20 to learn more about torches and

equipment.) Hold the glass in the flame until it is covered with a black carbon deposit (photo 2), then gradually add oxygen until the carbon begins to burn off (photo 3). Continue to hold the object at the end of the flame, rotate it around, and move it back and forth for a couple of minutes (photo 4).

To anneal larger borosilicate objects, place them in the kiln at room temperature, and heat it up to the annealing temperature as quickly as the kiln allows. The size and thickness of the object will determine the specific length of time that you need to hold the annealing temperature—a process known as *soaking*. Soaking for 30 minutes is sufficient for most pieces.

All borosilicate must be soaked at the annealing temperature of 1050°F (566°C). Borosilicate glass is so forgiving that, if something is well made, it can be put right into a hot kiln from room temperature without it cracking.

Before you anneal a piece made with borosilicate, train yourself to see any creases in areas where it has been twisted or hasn't been completely fused together. You must polish out these areas at the molten stage rather than the cooled stage. No amount of annealing will prevent cracking that can happen if you don't eliminate creases.

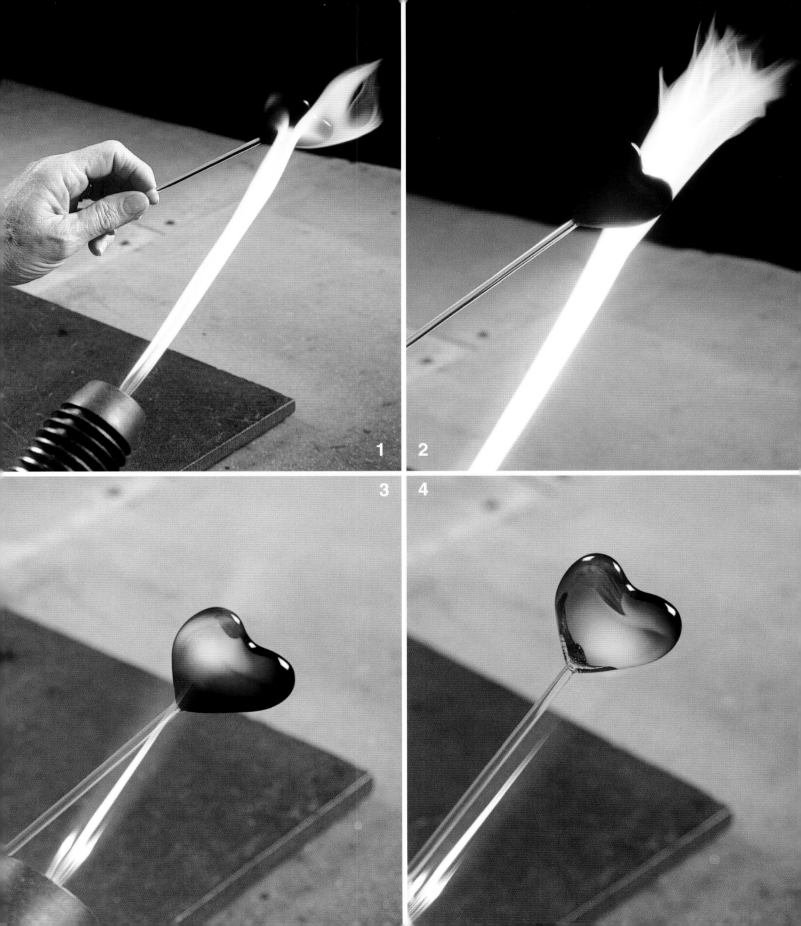

setting up your studio

Setting up a flameworking studio is relatively simple, inexpensive, and doesn't require a lot of space. If you want to work with hot glass, flameworking is an accessible way to begin experimenting.

Since you'll be working with an open flame, you'll need to put safety issues at the top of your list. You must have a flameproof floor and a flameproof surface on your workbench as well as good ventilation. (In essence, you should make everything in your studio as flameproof as possible.) Check with your local fire marshal for regulations that may apply. If you are setting up a studio in your home, you should also check your homeowner's insurance policy to make sure that you're within the restrictions of your policy.

The following sections describe equipment and tools that apply to your studio.

The author's studio built specifically for flameworking. (A smaller space works just as well for a beginner.)

For safety, secure oxygen tanks to a wall with chain or heavy chord.

general equipment

The items listed and described below are essential to your studio setup. Talk to your flameworking supplier about any unanswered questions that come up as you equip your studio.

oxygen tanks

You can buy or rent oxygen tanks in different sizes from your local oxygen supplier. You may not use a lot of oxygen when you're beginning to do flameworking, so a smaller-sized tank may suffice. As you work more, you may want to invest in a larger one. (It's convenient to have two or three tanks delivered at a time, and reorder when you begin to use up the last full tank. This way, you'll always have a full backup tank.)

Talk with the supplier about a system that fits your budget. Once your studio is set up, and you begin to do a lot of work, oxygen will be the most expensive part of your studio operation, because you'll use it fairly quickly.

Oxygen itself is not flammable, but because it causes things to burn, it can create a highly combustible situation. Pay attention to safety measures for storing and using it. You can store the tanks in your studio or put them in an easily accessible place outside where they are protected from the weather. Always position them upright and secure them with chains or chords to prevent them from falling over—an oxygen tank can become a torpedo capable of great damage if it falls and the valve on top is damaged.

To prevent a flammable situation, never store any kind of oil, oily rags, or oily equipment near your oxygen tanks. NEVER put oil on the cap of the oxygen tank which is screwed on to protect the valve, no matter how tempting it may seem if you're trying to screw off a cap that is stuck or rusted. Instead, be patient and work with it until you can get it to move in the right direction. If needed, wrap tape around the cap to assist you in loosening it, or use a rubber mallet and chisel to tap against the hole in the cap to help unscrew it.

Safety tip: Anytime you're going to be away from your torch for some time, you should turn off the oxygen at the tank and bleed, or empty, the line from the tank to your torch. To do this, turn off the tank before opening the oxygen valve on your torch. You'll hear a whooshing noise until all the oxygen is gone from the line. Then turn the oxygen valve on your torch to the off position.

oxygen regulator

You'll need an oxygen regulator that is in good/safe working condition for the top of your oxygen tank. You can purchase one through your local oxygen supplier. The regulator has two gauges: one gauge that tells you the gas pressure in the tank and indicates the amount of gas left, and an adjustable gauge with a dial that specifies the pressure of the oxygen going to the torch (measured in pounds per square inch [2.54 cm] or p.s.i.). Each torch has an optimal pressure requirement, so you'll need to set the adjustable dial to meet the requirements of the one you're using (torches are discussed in more detail later in this section).

To engage the oxygen regulator, screw it to the threaded valve on

top of the oxygen tank by hand before tightening it with a crescent wrench. To prevent leaks, tighten it on the brass fitting until snug. However, be aware that overtightening can strip the threads, wear down the fitting, and cause permanent damage.

If this happens, you might be able to use Teflon tape (available in the plumbing department of home supply stores) to get a snug fit. When using tape, wrap it around the male fitting of the threaded joint in the direction of the threaded turn. Then, when you screw the female fitting on, you won't unwind the tape. If this doesn't work, you may need to replace the regulator.

After the system is pressurized, test it for leaks by filling a spray bottle with a diluted solution of liquid made for this purpose (purchased through an oxygen supplier). Spray all of the fittings. If the liquid bubbles, there are leaks. Turn off everything and tighten those joints. (You may need to use Teflon tape or replace parts that leak.) It is important that you remember to take this step. For safety reasons, you MUST not use a system with leaks in it.

To turn on your tank, first set the adjustable gauge at zero before turning on the oxygen at the tank. (When you do this, turn your face away from the gauge. If a gauge should give way due to sudden pressure, it could explode.) The tank gauge will then register the pressure in the tank. At this point, you can turn the adjustable gauge to the correct pressure for the torch that you're using.

When you've finished using your torch, turn the screw valve for the oxygen tank to the off position. Open the oxygen valve on your torch to release pressure (bleed) in the line. Turn the adjustable gauge to zero.

If you have questions after reading this, talk with your oxygen supplier to learn how to attach the regulator and how to adjust the pressures.

A propane tank with regulator

propane tanks

Small propane tanks, such as one sized for an outdoor grill or smaller, are just right for flameworking. You can buy them at your local hardware store.

You won't use up propane as quickly as oxygen. The regulator for propane may have only one gauge for adjusting the gas pressure to the torch (see the next section for more information). If this is the case, the only means of telling how much propane is left in the tank is to weigh the tank. It's advisable to keep a backup tank handy.

Propane is highly flammable and MUST be stored outside. (If a leak should develop on your tank, it is unsafe for your studio.) Because propane tanks are smaller with a lower center of gravity than oxygen tanks, they're less likely to tip over. Nevertheless, it's still a good idea to secure them with a chain or chord to a wall as an extra precaution.

Safety tip: Anytime you're going to be away from your torch for some time, you'll need to bleed the line from the propane tank to your torch. To do this, turn off the oxygen first, then turn off the propane valve at the tank before turning on the torch's propane valve. Light the torch so that it continues to burn until all the propane is gone from the line. When the flame has burned out, turn off the propane valve at your torch. Then bleed the oxygen line. As the oxygen leaves the line, it will help to disseminate any residual propane.

propane regulator

The propane regulator for the top of your propane tank should also be in good working condition in order to be safe. Available through your oxygen supplier, this regulator is equipped with a safety device—a left-hand thread. Most threaded devices are designed to tighten down when turned in a right-hand (clockwise) direction, but the propane regulator is designed to turn in a left-hand (counterclockwise) direction when attaching it to the tank or *flashback arrestor* (see description on page 16). This counterclockwise turn is a wonderful safety feature that keeps you from connecting the regulator to anything other than a propane tank.

The propane regulator may have only one gauge, and you can adjust the pressure to the torch with the set dial. Each torch has an optimal, required pressure.

To attach the regulator to the propane tank, screw it to the fitting on top of the tank with a left-hand turn. Use the same technique that you used to fit the regulator on the oxygen tank: turn it with your hands before using a crescent wrench to screw it until it fits snugly while avoiding stripping the threads on the brass fitting. If you do strip the threads, you may be able to create a snug fit with Teflon tape, or you may need to replace the regulator.

Test for leaks in the same way that you would an oxygen tank—by spraying a liquid made for this purpose on all of the fittings. If there are leaks, turn everything off and tighten the fittings that are leaking. You may need to use Teflon tape, or use a new fitting, in order to eliminate the leak.

To set the pressure for the torch, turn the propane valve off at the torch, open the screw valve on top of the propane tank, and adjust the set dial to the correct pressure. Now you can open the valves at the torch and light it. When you've finished using your torch, turn the tank's screw valve to the off position. Turn on your torch's propane valve and light it. Bleed the line by allowing the torch to burn until all the gas is gone from the line and the flame extinguishes. Then turn the propane valve on your torch to the off position.

If you have further questions, talk with your professional propane supplier to learn how to attach the regulator and set the pressure.

flashback arrestors

These devices are attached to your oxygen and propane systems between the regulators and the hoses to prevent gases from flowing backwards. You'll need one that turns to the right for the oxygen system, and one that turns to the left for propane.

hoses

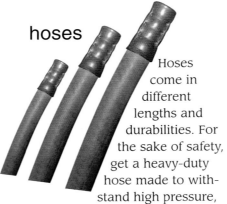

Hoses come in different lengths and durabilities. For the sake of safety, get a heavy-duty hose made to withstand high pressure, even though you may never use pressure as high as the hose is made to handle. These hoses are specifically designed to be used with oxygen and propane tanks, and they can be purchased from your oxygen or flameworking supplier. Also, get one that is suited in length for your setup—a lot of extra length in a hose is not a good idea because it can get in the way and cause a tripping accident.

This particular type of hose is actually two hoses in one (a red one and a green one) that are attached to each other side-by-side and can be pulled apart when necessary. Always attach the RED hose to PROPANE or natural gas and the GREEN hose to OXYGEN.

One end of the red hose has a fitting attached to it that screws onto your propane tank regulator or flashback arrestor with a LEFT-HAND turn. The green hose has a fitting that screws onto the oxygen tank regulator or flashback arrestor with a

RIGHT-HAND turn. Tighten the fittings so they're snug without stripping the threads. Use Teflon tape if the fittings are damaged, or replace them.

The other ends of the hose attach to your torch, which has a special fitting for this purpose: red to the fitting that supplies propane and green to the fitting that supplies oxygen. Usually the hose slips into the torch fitting. Make sure that it's all the way on when you fit it. Use hose clamps to firmly attach the hoses to your torch.

Safety tip: Make sure all your attachments are well fitted and don't leak. To test for leaks, use a spray liquid made for that purpose. Turn off the valves for both the propane and oxygen at your torch before turning on the valves at both tanks. Adjust the dial to the pressure you'll be using or slightly higher. Spray all the areas where parts of the system are attached to one another in both the propane and oxygen systems. If there are leaks, you'll see foamy bubbles. Turn everything off and make the necessary adjustments until no bubbles appear when you test the system again. You may need to tighten fittings with Teflon tape, secure them, or replace them.

workbench

You'll need a sturdy workbench for flameworking. You can make your own or have it built for you. It should be attached to the floor to prevent it from moving if someone bumps into it. (Depending on the type of floor that you have, you can use screws, bolts, angle irons, custom metal fittings, or other means of attachment.)

Choose a workbench size that accomodates your equipment: torch, tools, and the glass that you'll put on it. Some flameworkers prefer an "L" configuration because everything is within reach while they're working. How you set up your working surfaces is a personal preference, so visit the studios of other flameworkers for ideas if you have the opportunity. Try an arrangement, and if you don't like it, keep moving it until your workbench is comfortable for you.

The height of your workbench will be determined by how tall you are. You'll need a height that allows you to be able to move around and stand as you work, or sit in an adjustable chair. To save your muscles, joints, and ligaments, it's a good idea to change positions frequently.

The workbench should have enough space surrounding it to allow for a quick escape if you need to avoid getting burned by hot glass that drops from the table. Don't position your work-

A workbench made in an "L" configuration is very practical for flameworking.

bench so close to a wall that it prevents you from leaving easily. If your workbench is close to a wall, you'll need to cover the wall with fireproof material such as drywall or cement board. If your studio area is limited in size, face the wall and work with an open space at your back.

Whatever the size of the workbench that you configure, you MUST cover it in fireproof material. You can choose from different materials with different price ranges.

Cement board: This material, commonly used for flooring under tiles or slate, is available at home supply stores. It is made

from cement with a fibrous support structure. Mark the pieces of board to fit the top of your table, then score it with a utility knife before breaking it along the lines. Attach it with screws to your workbench. (You can also buy a type of special cement board through a flameworking supplier.)

Stainless or galvanized steel: Some flameworkers use stainless or galvanized steel as the work surface for the top of their workbenches. Though more expensive than cement board, this material is ideal for flameworking and is dust free. Contact a local sheet-metal contractor to get a top fabricated that fits your workbench.

workbench chair

To go with your workbench, choose a comfortable chair that has rollers and an adjustable height. Office supply and furniture stores are good places to look. The rollers allow you to quickly push yourself away from the workbench in an emergency, and this is an absolute necessity for your safety.

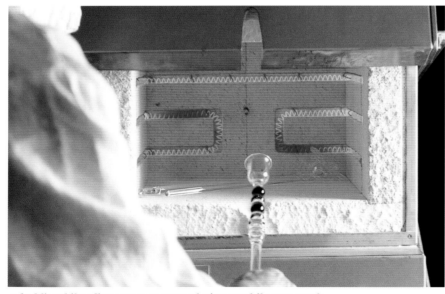

A holding kiln allows you to anneal pieces while you work.

holding kiln

Even though there are flameworkers who don't use a holding kiln, it is a very important piece of studio equipment because it allows you to preheat parts before attaching them to a more complex structure. It also allows

you to work on sculptural objects in stages. It is built with a cantilevered door that has a slotted hole in the bottom of the door for accomodating glass rods. The size of the piece that you make is limited by the kiln's interior. Small holding kilns are available from flameworking suppliers.

Check your electrical circuit before you install a kiln to make sure that you won't overload the circuit. You may need to hire an electrician to install a separate line for your kiln(s). Holding kilns are

available with digital controllers. Your flameworking supplier can help you decide on a system that best suits your needs.

The kiln is made to hold the pieces as they are in process and bring them up to annealing tem-

perature needed for the glass that you're using. Before inserting a piece, attach a glass rod to it, and, as it cools, place it in the back of the kiln with the rod extended out. You can plug the slot in the door with a piece of ceramic fiber board or ceramic cloth made for kiln use. The extended rod won't conduct heat, allowing you to remove and work with the piece(s) as needed. You can repeat this procedure as many times as needed.

ventilation system

Since noxious gases are a result of flameworking, you need a system for removing the gases and replenishing fresh air. Your flamework supplier may be able to advise you in this area, or you can consult an air specialist. Never work in a flameworking studio unless you have an adequate exchange of air.

A good ventilation system in your studio is a necessity for flameworking.

The ventilation system usually consists of a hood over your torch with an exhaust fan attached to it. You should also have fresh air coming into your studio at all times via a fan or other system. Don't use an exhaust fan without also providing some source of fresh outside air.

When you're finished working in the studio, leave the ventilation system running for a short period of time to clear the air.

protective eyewear

You MUST wear protective eyewear when flameworking. This is not optional, it is ESSENTIAL for the protection of your eyes. The glare from molten borosilicate glass, and especially from the colored glass, is very intense. A number of different types of protective glasses that eliminate sodium flare, infrared glare, and ultraviolet rays emitted from molten glass are available on the market.

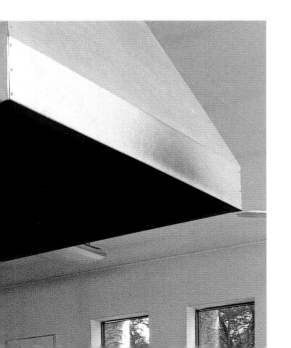

ALWAYS wear protective eyewear when flameworking.

Consult with your flameworking supplier to decide on glasses that fit the work you plan to do. Don't fudge on this piece of equipment—buy a good pair of glasses.

torch

The torch that you buy will be the most important piece of equipment that you invest in. As a beginner, you might consider learning to flamework with a smaller, less expensive torch before investing in a larger one. Most of the exercises in this book can be made with a small to midrange-sized torch. (If you decide later that you want to do a lot of glass blowing at the torch, you can invest in a larger torch.)

There are two types of torches: *internal mix torches* and *surface mix torches*. An internal mix torch is just what it sounds like— propane and oxygen are mixed together in the body of the torch so that they're projected together. This type of torch is often used as a hand torch for finish work.

There are lots of different tips made for internal mix torches that can be screwed onto the flame end. The tips vary from single holes of differing diameters to multiple holes. Some glass artists use these torches for sculpting as well as for finish work. They are versatile and affordable. To use this type of torch as a bench torch, you can install it in a weighted stand made for that purpose. (Buy this stand when you purchase your torch.)

A surface mix torch is designed so that the two types of gas move through the body of the torch separately before being mixed at the

A good torch is the most important piece of equipment that you'll buy.

surface. These types of torches, available in a large range of sizes and prices, are preferred by many artists because they are quiet and more versatile.

If you buy this kind of torch, you'll have to do some research to decide which one to purchase. Talk to your flameworking supplier about torch options, and, preferably, try them out before making a decision.

> **Safety tip:** No matter which type of torch you use, it must be securely attached to the surface of your workbench with a stand, screws, bolts, metal strapping material, or a large C-clamp. The torch should never fall off your workbench while lighted since it could start a fire or burn you.

first aid kit

Your first aid kit should contain ointments and bandages for use if you have minor cuts or burn yourself. An aloe plant is handy to have around for quick burn treatment. See a doctor immediately if you are unlucky enough to be inflicted with a severe burn or cut.

fire extinguisher

Check with your local fire department or fire marshal about the correct size and type of fire extinguisher for your studio. Small fire extinguishers are available in hard-ware supply stores. Get it inspected regularly and don't allow the contents to go out of date. It's a good idea to place two extinguishers in different and accessible spots in your studio.

"dropoff" bucket

This fireproof container is used for the disposal of hot bits of glass while you're working at the torch. (Always drop the pieces in the bucket, not on your work surface.) You can use a large tin can or a small galvanized bucket purchased at a home supply store for this purpose.

galvanized garbage can

When your dropoff bucket is full, empty the glass into a galvanized metal garbage that can be purchased at a home supply store. NEVER put anything but glass into this can, or it could start a fire.

protective high-temperature gloves

Oftentimes, it is easier to work on an object if you can hold the piece in your hands, especially when making larger pieces. For picking up and holding pieces of hot glass, you'll need a pair of high-temperature gloves from a flameworking supplier. You'll also use these gloves to put pieces into the kiln and take them out.

Fire extinguisher, protective glasses, and high-temperature gloves

fireproof studio floor

The floor of your workspace must be flameproof. The ideal situation is a space with a concrete floor that can be occasionally hosed down with water to clean it. Since this is not always possible, cover other kinds of floors underneath work areas with a material that meets the fire safety codes for your region. Use a nonflammable, nonporous material such as slate or ceramic tile. Remove any paper or flammable materials to prevent fires. To keep from stirring up glass dust—a definite safety hazard—wet mop the floor to keep it clean, rather than sweeping it.

Tools for shaping and manipulating hot glass. (Left to right, clockwise: Tungsten pick, graphite reamers in two different sizes, graphite plates, graphite rods in various diameters, parallel press/smasher, flat travel iron, glass-cutting scissors, graphite paddles in two different sizes, old dinner knives, tweezers in two different sizes)

tools

When you equip your studio, you'll begin adding tools as you need them. The following tools are all used in the exercises and projects of this book.

specialized tools

These tools are specifically designed for use in flameworking.

flint lighter/hand striker: Use this tool to ignite your torch. Always use a flint lighter instead of some of the other igniters that aren't safe. Keep replacement flints handy.

glass scoring knife: This knife is used to scratch the surface of a glass rod or tube so that you can break it down into useable lengths.

graphite rods: These rods, available through a flameworking supplier, come in various diameters and are used for manipulating the glass. The ends are flat, but you can make them round or pointed by using a pencil sharpener or rubbing the end against sandpaper. Try out several in different diameters until you find out which ones you use the most.

graphite paddle: This rectangular paddle, used for shaping the glass, has an attached handle. Begin by supplying your studio with a medium-sized one. Larger paddles can also be used as a plate for maneuvering the glass.

graphite plates: Flat graphite plates are placed on your workbench to protect the surface and hold pieces of hot glass. They can also be used to shape and form the glass. They usually come in sizes of 6 x 12 inches (15.2 x 30.5 cm) and 12 x 12 inches (30.5 x 30.5 cm). Start out with a couple of plates, and add more if you need them.

octagonal-shaped graphite reamers: These pointed tools with handles are made of tapered pieces of graphite in various diameters. They're used to shape glass loops and open glass tubing. Get a large one (10 mm to 25 mm) and a small one (2 mm to 12 mm).

tweezers: These large stainless steel tweezers made for flameworking can be purchased from a flameworking supplier. (Sometimes you can find used tweezers at flea markets or swap meets.) Equip your studio with an 8-inch-long (20.3 cm) and 12-inch-long (30.5 cm) pair. They have many uses, but the most important is removing molten glass from areas where you don't want it as you're working on a piece.

tungsten pick: This tool, used for manipulating the glass, is composed of a pointed piece of tungsten attached to a handle. One is all that you'll need to begin with.

finger tool/claw holder: These tools that come in various sizes are made to hold glass objects made from opened tubing. If you want to make simple blown objects, you'll need one made to hold objects from approximately 1 inch (2.5 cm) in diameter to 3 to 4 inches (7.6-10.2 cm) in diameter.

parallel press/smasher: This tool, composed of two flat metal plates attached to one another with a U-shaped handle, is made for smashing molten glass into a disc with parallel sides. This is not an essential tool when you're beginning flameworking, but it's really nice to have.

glass-cutting scissors: These scissors from a flameworking supplier are made to cut hot glass. Buy a size that fits comfortably in your hand.

markers: Permanent markers are great for drawing cut lines on glass. Even after the color from the flame burns off the glass, the mark remains on it.

steel ruler: You'll need a ruler to measure rods and parts that you assemble.

pens and pencils: Keep standard pens and pencils on hand for drawing, sketching, and taking notes.

utility knife: You may need this tool to cut thick paper or foamcore into patterns.

"found" and miscellaneous tools

You can find some of these adapted tools in your kitchen, garage, or tool box.

wide-bladed dinner knife: A stainless steel dinner knife that has parallel edges is invaluable for shaping and forming hot glass. Look for one at a thrift store, flea market, antique store, or other sources that carry used dinnerware.

paring knife: A stainless steel paring knife is great to have on hand for shaping and forming glass. Use the fine point and edge to create details in the molten glass.

small, flat travel iron: This small, heavy iron with no holes on the bottom might be a bit challenging to locate, but it makes a perfect tool for smashing large amounts of molten glass. Check out antique shops or flea markets, search the Web, and look through auctions on the Internet.

wooden block with drilled holes: Use a piece of 2 x 4 about 8 to 10 inches (20.3-25.4 cm) long to make a block for holding rods of different sizes. Place the block of wood on its wide side, and use drill bits of various sizes to make holes in the top about halfway through the block.

crescent wrench: Use this common tool for screwing regulators on and off oxygen and propane tanks. You'll need to buy an adjustable wrench or a large one for the tank fittings and a smaller one for other fittings.

level: You'll use a small carpenter's level (about 6 to 8 inches [15.2-20.3 cm] long) to gauge whether related parts of objects are level horizontally and vertically.

brass brush: Use this brush for cleaning the surface of your torch. Since brass is a soft metal, it won't harm the torch's metal. This item can be purchased at a hardware store or through a flameworking supplier.

bench brush: Any kind of wide and soft brush can be used to clean your bench. A flat paintbrush works well for this purpose.

dust pan and brush: Use a soft brush and pan to sweep away dust and glass bits off your workbench. Always sweep very gently to avoid creating hazardous dust.

healing, "devit," creases, and cracks

After you've been working with the glass for a while, you will probably notice a few out-of-the-ordinary things about the pieces that you've made.

For instance, there might be places on the surface of the glass that have a white, frosted look. Or, you might have missed creases that needed healing, leading to cracking in the glass. You might see cracks running into the body of a piece. The section that follows gives you insight into why such surprises occur and how to fix them.

devitrification

What does it mean to say that glass is amorphous? When a substance is described as amorphous, it implies that it lacks a crystalline structure. However, under certain circumstances, glass will form crystals on the surface of the clear glass that make it appear frosted.

In several of the exercises, you'll take the glass out of the flame, and hold it perfectly still until the glass sets up. If you move borosilicate glass at all during this period in which it is becoming solid again, crystals will form and manifest themselves, creating a frosted area on the surface of the glass. This crystallization is called *devitrification*—shortened to "devit" by glass professionals.

Devitrification is not structurally damaging or weakening to the glass, but it is unsightly. (If you want a frosted effect, you can produce it another way, such as by sandblasting.) If you have devitrified spots on your glass, they shout that you are technically unskilled. Watch for devitrification while you're making a piece, and fire-polish it away while the piece is still very hot.

Check your finished pieces for devitrified areas after making them. Fortunately, it's simple to get rid of devit by melting the glass again in these areas. To do this, get a good grip on the glass (you may need to reattach a *punty*—a short rod for holding the piece) and make sure that the piece is warmed in the crystallized area at the end of the flame (photo 1). Once the piece has been warmed sufficiently, place it directly in the flame where the area is located (photo 2). Hold the piece still until you see the surface cloudiness disappear. As the surface gets hot, you should see it rapidly turn from a frosted area to a highly polished one (photo 3). Take it out of the flame, hold it perfectly still, and allow the glass to become solid again (photo 4).

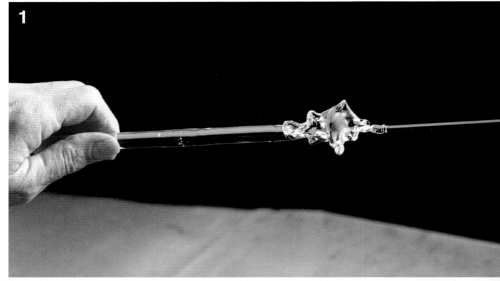

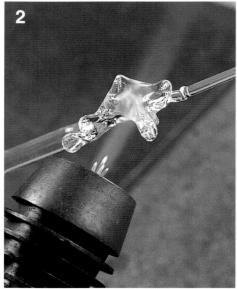

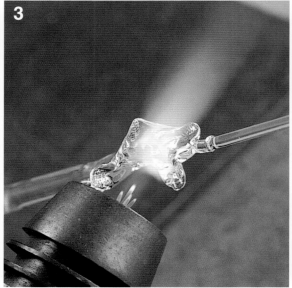

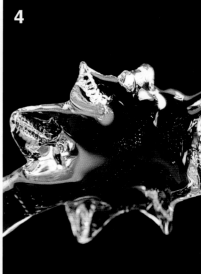

creases

Creases are the bane of the beginning flameworker, and it's very difficult to work with the glass without them appearing. You can't always prevent them from happening, but you can learn to recognize them and have the patience to work with the glass until they're gone.

If you have trouble seeing them, use a knife and run the blade along the surface of the glass. Anywhere that the blade of the knife gets caught along the surface, there's a crease that needs repair.

Creases happen most frequently in areas where two pieces of glass have been stuck together—whether from adding dots, stripes, or a new part to the piece that you're working on (photo 5). The best way of preventing creases in the first place is to make certain that your glass is hot and fluid on both surfaces before you stick the two pieces of glass together. Twisting the glass while working on it can also create creases.

You can remove creases by fire-polishing them, but it must be done carefully so that they don't start a crack that runs through the glass. There are several steps to fire-polishing out a crease:

1. Warm the area of the crease by holding the piece out at the END of the flame for several minutes. If you don't warm the glass before you put it in the flame, the sudden heat shock will cause a crack to form in the area of the crease. (If you have a holding kiln, you can

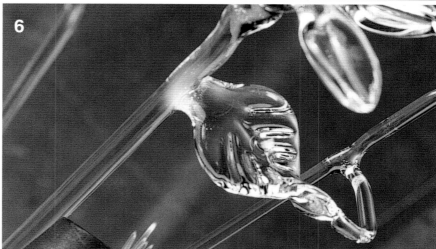

put the piece in for several minutes to saturate it with heat. Naturally, any heating process you use will take longer if the piece is thick.)

2. Once the piece has been sufficiently warmed, get a good grip on the piece before holding the crease in the flame. Hold it still until you see the glass flow together over the crease. Remove

it from the flame, hold it perfectly still, and allow the glass to become solid again so that it sets up. In the process of doing this, you'll need to hold the glass with two hands or make sure it is well-supported by a bridge system (see page 81) to prevent the glass from moving as it is setting up (photo 6).

The process of removing a crease can be compared to this: A crease is like a valley between two mountains. When the sun shines, the tops of the mountains are bathed in sunlight and warm up long before the shaded valley. When the sun gets high enough, it warms the valley.

In other words, when you heat an area of glass that has a crease, the highest areas will heat up first and begin to glow before the deeper, darker one does. As the surrounding glass gets hotter and hotter it will begin to flow. You'll eventually see it flow into the darker area of the crease. When the crease fills with molten glass, the entire area will glow with the same intensity of color. Creases are easier to discern in clear glass than in colored glass.

3. If a crease runs all the way around a glass part that you've joined to another one (for instance, a leaf added to a stem with the crease circling around the joint), you'll have to heal the crease in this order: the top of the joint, the bottom, one side, and then the other side. Take the glass out of the flame after each step, hold it perfectly still, and let it become solid again before you proceed to the next step. This process is a lot of work, but it's absolutely necessary. (Of course, the best way to work is to learn to join two pieces of glass when they're hot enough so creases don't form in the first place.)

No amount of annealing will heal creases or prevent cracks from running. You MUST heal creases in the flame before the piece is annealed.

cracks

No matter how careful you are when you're creating a piece, you'll eventually get cracks in your work. In these areas, the glass has separated just enough to allow the entrance of air, which has different optical characteristics than glass. Cracks can be caused by several different things.

Creases are a definite cause of cracks. Usually, the piece you've added won't crack and break off (although it can happen), but the crease can cause a crack to run into the body of the piece.

Sometimes cracks will also form if the *heat differential* is too great. If a piece you've made has cooled to room temperature, it is essentially cold. If you thrust that glass directly into the flame, it will heat up a spot surrounded by cold glass. The differences in temperature will be too great, and as the glass cools, it will crack from heat shock. This is why the exercises will tell you to warm the piece out at the end of the flame before putting it into the hotter portion.

This is especially true if the glass has not been annealed. If the glass is warmed before you put it in the flame, the heat differential will be less, and the chance of it cracking diminishes.

Surface cracks have a telltale crackly appearance that resembles a spider web. If you heat the surface of the glass but don't bring it to red hotness, the surface tension is released as the glass cools, and cracks form. This usually happens when you're concentrating on working in one area with the flame and don't notice that it has brushed another part of the surface.

To heal any types of cracks, first warm the glass out at the end of a soft, bushy flame or place it in a holding kiln. If you're dealing with surface cracks, hold the cracked area underneath the flame and slowly bring it up into the flame. Heat the affected area until you see the cracks flow together, and the glass glows from red to white. This will probably leave a pattern of small, trapped air bubbles that form lines where the cracks were.

To get rid of crack lines, heat the glass to a red-hot state again before it cools. Then use your tweezers to carefully extract small bits of glass where the lines are. You can also remove lines with the end of a cold glass rod. To do this, heat the glass to a red-hot state, remove it from the flame, and pull out the lined area by touching it with the rod to pull the molten glass away.

You might need to do this several times before enough of the glass is removed, leaving a depressed area in the glass. If this happens, you can fill the depression by heating an area adjacent to it to

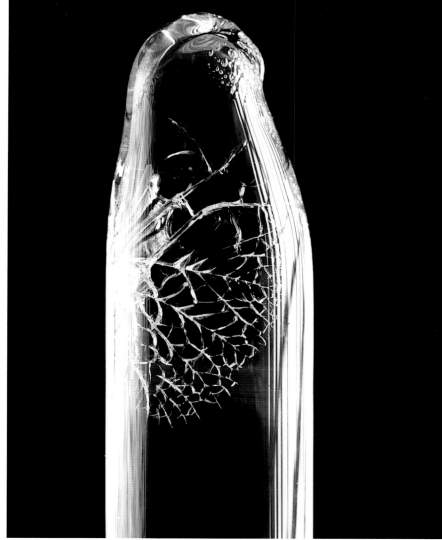

Surface cracks have a telltale crackly appearance that resembles a spider web.

heating the glass so it flows together to heal the crack. To take advantage of gravity, hold the piece so the crack runs vertically and the molten glass flows down into the crack.

If air gets trapped in the glass, keep heating the glass from different angles until the glass around the trapped air is molten enough to allow a round bubble to form. If the air is trapped deep within a piece, this heating process may take quite some time. Continually check the area of trapped air until you can see the bubble. Unless it is large, it won't be very noticeable.

A nicely rounded bubble will also prevent cracks from forming again, because pressure pushes in equally from all sides, and the bubble will be contained. (After you have done this with several pieces, you will learn which pieces are worth spending the time to repair and which ones simply need to be discarded.)

a red-hot state and allowing the glass to flow down into the place where you removed some glass.

To heal a crack that has run into the body of a piece, begin by warming up the glass. Hold it out at the end of a narrow, soft flame, and heat only the area of glass that is immediately around the crack. Gradually bring the glass down into the flame, heating only

the end of the crack that is deepest into the body of the piece.

To avoid trapping air in the glass, heat the crack from the inside out to the edge. Your aim is to soften the glass at the inside end of the crack, so it can't run farther into the body of the piece. Once you've softened that inside end, begin to work from side to side toward the outside edge,

> **Caution:** If air is trapped in the glass, it can cause it to break if you allow it to cool and try to reheat it— even if it is annealed. Air expands much faster than glass when heated, and if you plunge a piece of glass with trapped air into the flame without warming it first, it may explode.

color, glorious color!

When you work with colored glass, it opens up a whole new range of creative possibilities that require additional skills. This section introduces you to the basics of color.

Since the exercises and projects in this book are made exclusively with borosilicate glass, you'll use borosilicate color as well. This is a wonderful time to work with colored borosilicate glass. More companies are beginning to make colored borosilicate, and the available range of colors continues to grow.

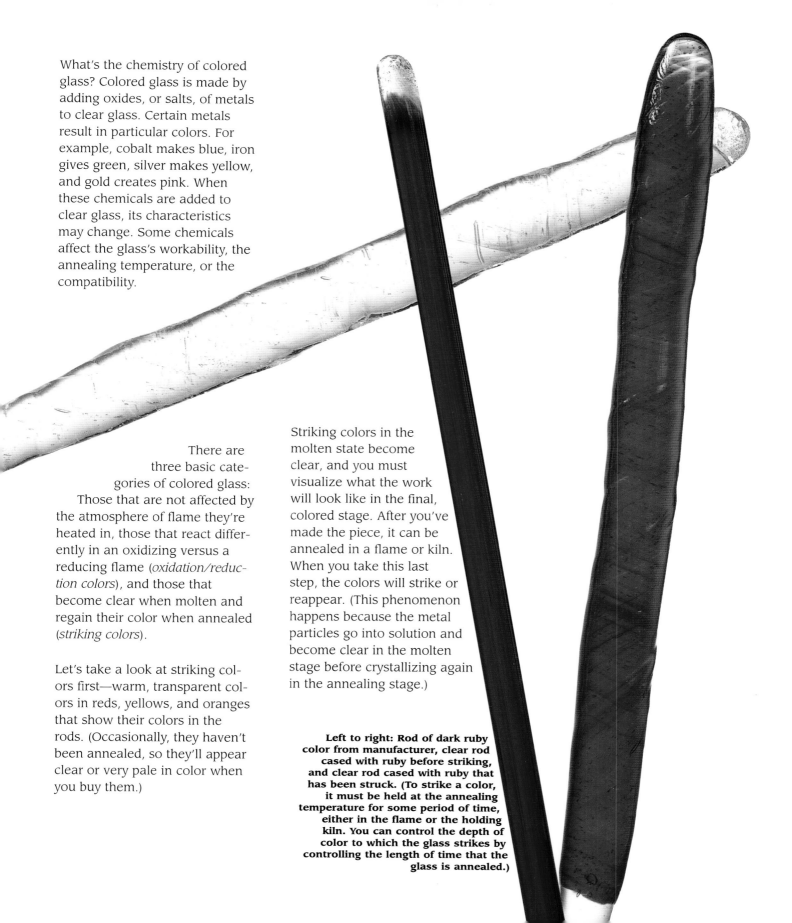

What's the chemistry of colored glass? Colored glass is made by adding oxides, or salts, of metals to clear glass. Certain metals result in particular colors. For example, cobalt makes blue, iron gives green, silver makes yellow, and gold creates pink. When these chemicals are added to clear glass, its characteristics may change. Some chemicals affect the glass's workability, the annealing temperature, or the compatibility.

There are three basic categories of colored glass: Those that are not affected by the atmosphere of flame they're heated in, those that react differently in an oxidizing versus a reducing flame (*oxidation/reduction colors*), and those that become clear when molten and regain their color when annealed (*striking colors*).

Let's take a look at striking colors first—warm, transparent colors in reds, yellows, and oranges that show their colors in the rods. (Occasionally, they haven't been annealed, so they'll appear clear or very pale in color when you buy them.)

Striking colors in the molten state become clear, and you must visualize what the work will look like in the final, colored stage. After you've made the piece, it can be annealed in a flame or kiln. When you take this last step, the colors will strike or reappear. (This phenomenon happens because the metal particles go into solution and become clear in the molten stage before crystallizing again in the annealing stage.)

Left to right: Rod of dark ruby color from manufacturer, clear rod cased with ruby before striking, and clear rod cased with ruby that has been struck. (To strike a color, it must be held at the annealing temperature for some period of time, either in the flame or the holding kiln. You can control the depth of color to which the glass strikes by controlling the length of time that the glass is annealed.)

The workability of striking colors isn't a lot different from that of clear glass—they're of the same consistency when they're heated and cooled. The chemicals used to make them don't affect compatibility either, but the annealing temperature may be slightly higher than that of clear glass.

Experiment with your annealing kiln to find the temperature setting that's best for getting the colors to strike to the preferred saturation. If you have difficulty getting them to strike, raise the temperature of your kiln a few degrees, or leave the glass in the kiln for a longer soak than for the clear glass. You can control the intensity of the color with temperature and time. Remember that the annealing temperature for clear borosilicate glass is 1050°F (566°C).

Oxidation/reduction colors are some of the most interesting of all of the borosilicate colors. These colors are very sensitive to the atmosphere of the flame you use when working with them. Earlier in the book, when the torch was introduced, you learned that a yellow flame is a reducing flame (low in oxygen), and a blue, active flame is an oxidizing flame (high in oxygen). The flame in between these two is a neutral flame. In this flame, neither gas dominates. Flames from yellow to neutral are in the reducing range, and flames from neutral to blue are in the oxidizing range.

The colors that you'll get when using oxidation/reduction colors are highly affected by the type of flame to which the glass is exposed, and some very interesting effects can result. You can work with these colors in a very uncontrolled way, allowing the colors to do their own thing as you work with them; or you can develop your knowledge about these colors, and learn to control them to get the effects you desire. Either approach is acceptable.

Think of the colors in the atmosphere of the flame in this way: The colors contain oxides of metals, and when you work them in an oxidizing flame, there is an abundance of oxygen surrounding the glass. Because of this situation, the chemical composition of the metal oxides doesn't really change (with the exception of

Left to right: An oxidation/reduction color and the results of the color cased onto a clear rod in an oxidizing flame.

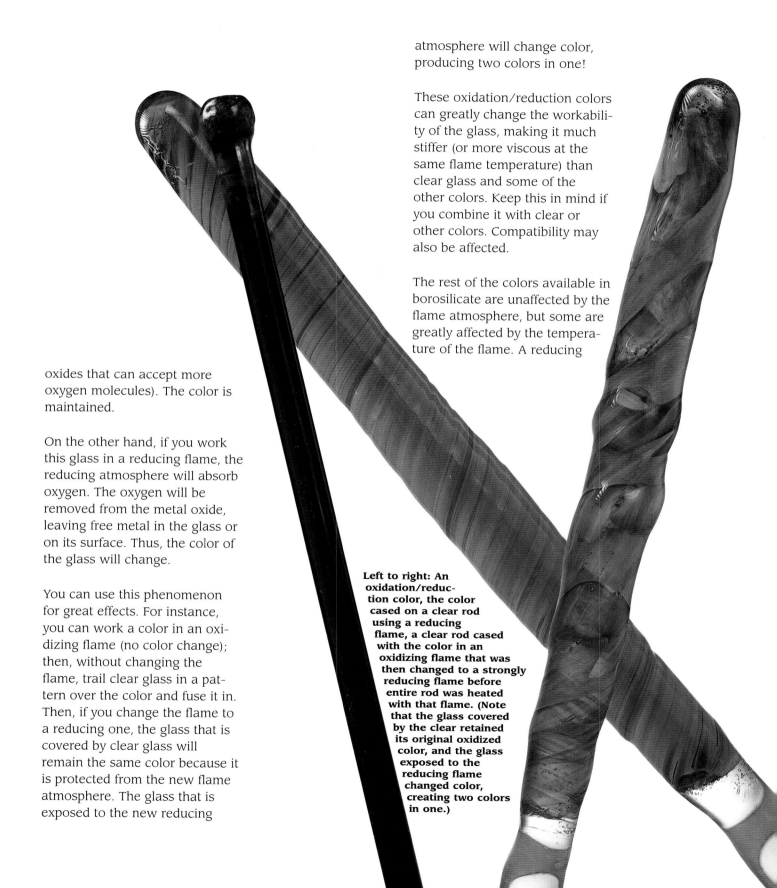

atmosphere will change color, producing two colors in one!

These oxidation/reduction colors can greatly change the workability of the glass, making it much stiffer (or more viscous at the same flame temperature) than clear glass and some of the other colors. Keep this in mind if you combine it with clear or other colors. Compatibility may also be affected.

The rest of the colors available in borosilicate are unaffected by the flame atmosphere, but some are greatly affected by the temperature of the flame. A reducing

oxides that can accept more oxygen molecules). The color is maintained.

On the other hand, if you work this glass in a reducing flame, the reducing atmosphere will absorb oxygen. The oxygen will be removed from the metal oxide, leaving free metal in the glass or on its surface. Thus, the color of the glass will change.

You can use this phenomenon for great effects. For instance, you can work a color in an oxidizing flame (no color change); then, without changing the flame, trail clear glass in a pattern over the color and fuse it in. Then, if you change the flame to a reducing one, the glass that is covered by clear glass will remain the same color because it is protected from the new flame atmosphere. The glass that is exposed to the new reducing

Left to right: An oxidation/reduction color, the color cased on a clear rod using a reducing flame, a clear rod cased with the color in an oxidizing flame that was then changed to a strongly reducing flame before entire rod was heated with that flame. (Note that the glass covered by the clear retained its original oxidized color, and the glass exposed to the reducing flame changed color, creating two colors in one.)

flame is a cool flame that becomes hotter as you add oxygen, but if you continue to add oxygen, the flame begins to cool down again. When working with this group of colors, experiment with flame temperature to decide which works best for each. (Some colors, for instance, will boil at high temperatures, causing an unwanted bubbly effect.)

Colored glass comes in a variety of forms: powders, frits, and rods. Powders and *frits* are simply crushed up glass in various grit sizes. The colored rods are short compared to the length of clear glass rods, and they come in different diameters. If you need rods with specific diameters, you can request those, but you'll pay extra for the sorting that's required.

Borosilicate colors are expensive when compared to those available in soft glass. Color is purchased by the pound, and a pound of colored rods is not a very big handful. For this reason, you can use techniques (such as casing a clear rod with color that you'll learn how to do later) to create the illusion of a lot of color. As a beginner, you may want to save yourself some money by buying seconds or odds colored rods—ones that

may have slight defects. When you're first beginning to work with color, you'll be doing a lot of experimenting, so these rods may be just right for you.

The various companies that make or supply colored borosilicate usually provide information about each of the colors and the category that it falls into. They also sell sample packs, so you can try out small amounts of each color before you commit to buying larger quantities.

Color cased onto a clear rod which has been unaffected by the atmosphere of the flame.

Glass tubing can be blown into small objects.

glass rods and tubing

In the first exercises in the book, you'll work only with solid glass rods of various diameters. Then you'll have the opportunity to learn to create objects at the torch with glass tubing, which will require a new set of skills and a lot of patience.

Working with tubing is very different from flameworking solid rods (see page 36 for more information about rods). When you're heating and forming a glass tube, the outside walls are supported only by the pressure of your breath. Working with glass tubing can be a tricky operation that takes a lot of practice, but you can achieve wonderful results.

Like glass rod, tubing comes in different diameters indicated by the outside walls. Because the walls of the hollow tubes can be of different thicknesses (indicated as standard, medium, or heavy), the inside diameter of tubes can vary, even if the outside is the same. For instance, if the wall is of standard (or the thinnest) thickness, the inside diameter will be greater than if the wall is heavy. This becomes important if you are trying to slide one size of tubing down into another.

A good all-purpose tubing to begin with is 25 mm, standard-wall tubing because it is relatively easy to hold and manipulate. This tubing can be made into objects such as candleholders, small blown cups, and flared feet for goblets or candleholders.

There are a couple of ways to prepare tubing for blowing. One is to close the end of the tubing, and then gather glass by heating it until you have enough to blow into the shape that you want.

The other way is to heat the tubing and pull what are called *"points."* Points are long, tapered sections of glass that are pulled from the tubing to serve as both handles and a blowpipe for the section of tubing between them. This unpulled area is what you'll heat and blow into an object.

In the exercise on page 89, you'll learn the technique called *"pulling points"* to work with tubing. Then you'll put that knowledge to work to make an object.

the exercises

In the following exercises, you'll learn to work with the glass and your torch as you make basic objects from borosilicate. These pieces will be assembled in the projects that follow the exercises. The shapes may seem simplistic at first, but with the mastery of each, your working knowledge will increase, building on your skills in preparation for the next.

The beauty of this way of learning is that you can work completely at your own pace. When you feel that you have mastered a series of skills, move on to the next. In the beginning, the instructions will be very detailed. In subsequent exercises, certain knowledge that you've gained will be assumed (such as how to make a ball on the end of a glass rod or how to attach a punty).

After building a basic vocabulary of shapes, you'll eventually use this lexicon to create your own interpretations in glass.

Flameworking is a lot of fun; however, it will take hours of working at your torch to develop your skills. As you spend your time at the torch, you'll get gratification from making some very nice things. At first, you'll have to look closely at everything you do in order to gauge what's happening. Later, as you've worked a lot with the glass, you'll be able to sense when you're doing it right.

Above all, give yourself permission to fail in the beginning. Don't expect perfection. Relax and have fun. Take a few deep breaths when you begin to work, and allow the Zen of glass to take over. When you make mistakes, view that failure as an opportunity for learning by analyzing what went wrong and how you can improve the next time you try the same thing. If you find that almost everything is going wrong, take a break, move around, and do some totally different activity for a while—then come back and begin again.

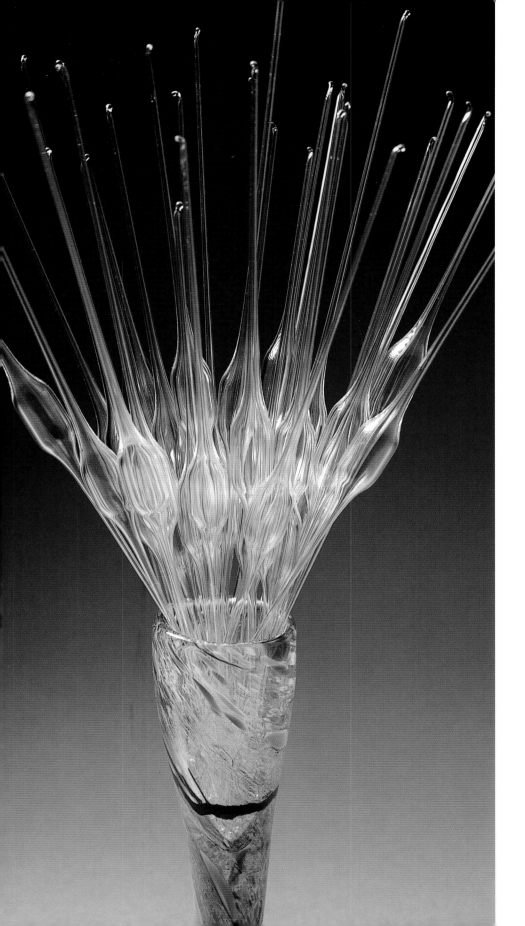

getting started

Most of the exercises that follow use clear borosilicate glass. If you've had experience working with soft glass but have never worked with borosilicate, you'll find it's a whole new experience. As a flameworker and a teacher, I always limit my students to clear glass while they are learning. Colored glass is fun, seductive, and expensive. As a beginner, you need to learn about the properties of glass and how to "read" it, form it, and fuse it before you begin adding color.

Annealing isn't mentioned in any of the following exercises, because you can practice making all of the objects from borosilicate, and allow them to cool to room temperature without annealing them. If you want to go ahead and anneal the pieces that you make, flame anneal them or anneal them in a holding kiln. If your pieces are cracking as they cool, you probably haven't eliminated all of the creases as you made them, or you've heat-shocked them in some way while making them.

In all of the instructions, you'll see the abbreviation of "D" to indicate the dominant hand and "ND" to indicate the nondominant hand. (If you're right-handed, your right will be the dominant hand and your left the nondominant hand. If you are left-handed, it will be the opposite.)

These exercises will also help you to find a scale that is comfortable for you. Some flameworkers are drawn to assembling large pieces, while others prefer working on a small and detailed scale.

cutting glass rods

If you buy glass rods by the case, they'll come in lengths that are impossible to use without shortening them. Smaller-diameter rods are easier to cut. Before you begin work at the torch, cut some lengths of rod.

To cut a rod, use a scoring knife equipped with a steel blade. This knife is not sharp enough to cut your finger, but it is sharp enough to scratch, or score, the surface of the glass without cutting it. The score line breaks the surface tension of the glass, and applied pressure breaks the glass cleanly. ALWAYS wear glasses to protect your eyes when cutting rods.

Try cutting several different diameters (such as 7 mm, 10 mm, and 12 mm) using the following steps:

1. Begin with a 12 mm rod, and hold it in your nondominant (ND) hand.

2. With your dominant (D) hand, place the cutter crossways underneath the rod with the sharp edge touching the rod (photo 1). Place your thumb on top of the rod just above the cutting edge (photo 2).

3. As you press hard with your thumb, draw the cutting edge across the diameter of the glass. You should be able to see the score line easily (photo 3). You may have to draw the blade more than once over the same spot to get a defined line.

4. On the opposite side of the rod from the score line, place your thumbs on either side of it, not directly over it (photo 4).

5. Press down on the rod with your thumbs, and push up with your fingers at the same time. The rod should break instantly, and the glass will break away from your face (photo 5). (If you've never done this before, you may feel a bit hesitant, but you'll be amazed at how easily the rod breaks.)

6. Use the same procedure with the other rods until you have at least two pieces of each size rod that measure around 12 to 15 inches (30.5-38.1 cm) long each.

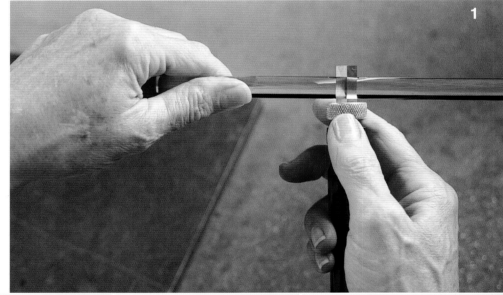

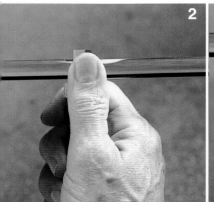
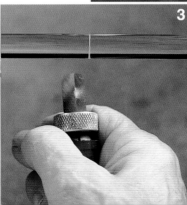
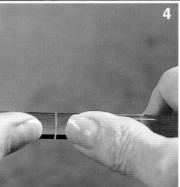
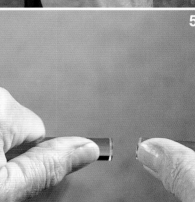

A torch allows you to place the heat exactly where it is needed.

operating your torch

Each kind of torch comes with its own specific instructions from the manufacturer that you should read and follow. However, some basic instructions apply to all torches that are used for flameworking.

When you begin, always turn the propane on first and light the torch before turning on the oxygen and adjusting the flame to the size and shape needed. (During the course of making even a simple piece, you may need to adjust the flame many times.)

Keep in mind that the heat does the work. The beauty of flameworking is that you can place heat exactly where needed to make the glass move as you wish. You may need a small flame with very sharp edges, a large flame with very bushy edges, or any number of variations in between these extremes.

Learning how to use a torch effectively is a major portion of the learning curve for a beginning flameworker. This process includes deciding where you need to apply the heat, how large an area needs to be heated, and how long the heat needs to be applied.

One of the dilemmas for the beginning flameworker is the fact that the glass needs to be extremely hot to move; but, as a beginner, you won't have the skills necessary to control the glass when it's molten. With experience, you'll learn to "read" the glass, so you can tell how hot it is by its color in the flame.

When you have only the yellow gas flame burning, this is known as a *reducing flame*. As you add more oxygen, the flame will turn from yellow to blue. When the gas and oxygen are fairly equally balanced, the flame becomes a *neutral flame*. If you continue to add more oxygen, the flame will get louder and more active.

When it reaches this stage, it is an *oxidizing flame*. If you continue to add oxygen, it may extinguish the flame. Being able to recognize different flames is very important, especially when you begin working with color.

> **Note:** There are degrees of reducing and oxidizing. For instance, when you add oxygen to a yellow flame and it turns blue, it is still a reducing flame until you have added enough oxygen for it to become a neutral flame. As you add more oxygen it becomes less reducing. This knowledge becomes useful when working with color.

The recommended method of lighting your torch is with a flint lighter/hand striker—a tool made for this purpose that you can purchase through a flameworking supplier. A small piece of flint rubs across a section of rough metal to create sparks for lighting the torch when you squeeze the striker's handle. You may feel

Flint lighter

awkward doing this at first, but it is safer than any other method.

Practice using the striker to create sparks before you light the torch, then hold the cup of the striker about ½ inch (1.3 cm) away from the end of the torch, and turn on the propane at a very low level. Squeeze the striker several times to create sparks until the torch lights (see photo above). You should have a small flame that is about 1 or 2 inches (2.5-5.1 cm) in length.

Caution: If the torch doesn't light within a few seconds, turn it off and wave your hands in front of it to dissipate any gas that might have escaped before you try again. Don't create a fireball!

Once the torch is lighted, you can adjust your flame by adding a bit of propane, followed by some oxygen. Alternate these up or down until you have the flame that you need for your project. (If the flame blows out at any point, turn everything off and begin again.)

In the first few exercises that follow this section, a description of the flame that you need to use and reminders to adjust it will guide you in the process of learning to use your torch.

Safety tips: Always turn the propane on first and off last. (To remember this, use the acronym, POOP: Propane on first, then Oxygen on; Oxygen off first, then Propane off.) NEVER leave your torch while it is burning. When you leave, make a habit of turning it off. When you return, turn it back on and adjust the flame.

testing for compatibility of glass

If you have an unidentified rod of glass, or you need to find out if two rods are compatible, here's a simple test which you can do to determine compatibility:

1. In the flame, stripe one rod onto about 1 inch (2.5 cm) of the other rod (photo 7). (See the exercise on page 64 to learn how to case a rod.)

2. Heat the area containing the stripe until it is molten (photo 8), and remove it from the flame.

3. Hold the rod vertically, grab the fused end with tweezers, and pull straight down to extract a thread of glass from the end of the two fused rods (photo 9).

4. While it cools, continue to hold the rod vertically with the thread attached.

5. If the glass is compatible, the thread will remain straight. If the two glasses are not compatible, the thread will curve (photo 10). The greater the curve, the more incompatible the glasses are. (By holding the glass vertically, you can be sure that any resulting curve is not from gravity.)

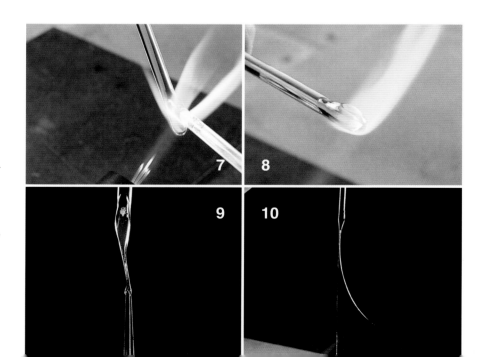

exercise 1—
MAKING GATHERS, EXPERIMENTING
WITH GRAVITY, AND FUSING RODS

Before you can begin making shapes from glass, you need to learn some basic ways of manipulating glass through the three parts of the exercise that follow. In this first exercise, as well as the two that follow, extra rods of different diameters are listed along with the size used in the instructions. After you've followed the instructions, try making the same piece from these rods to experience working with the other sizes.

making a gather 1

To create an object, you have to begin by making what is called a "gather" or ball of molten glass at the end of a rod. Before heating the rod, clean it with a soft cloth or paper towel saturated with a bit of rubbing alcohol or white vinegar. Any scratches, dust, finger oils, or other residue on the surface can cause bubbles to form when the glass is molten. When you use alcohol, make sure to keep it away from the flame.

experimenting with gravity 2

Once you've learned to make a gather or ball at the end of a rod, you'll experiment with gravity—your greatest tool as well as enemy in flameworking. Use gravity to bend rods, make glass flow in the direction needed to make shapes, thicken glass to form stronger structures, and fill in cracks or crevices. Eventually, this work will become so intuitive that you won't have to think about it.

fusing two rods end-to-end 3

As you use rods to create work, you'll end up with short pieces of glass. When a rod is 6 inches (15.2 cm) or smaller, it's not long enough to work with comfortably or in a controlled manner. Instead of throwing these pieces away, you can fuse them together to make longer ones that you can continue to use. This simple technique is described below.

materials

Clear borosilicate rods:

2, 7 mm x 12-15 inches (30.5-38.1 cm) long

2, 10 mm x 12-15 inches (30.5-38.1 cm) long

2, 12 mm x 12-15 inches (30.5-38.1 cm) long

tools

Tweezers

making a gather 1

1. To practice turning the rod, hold one of the 7 mm rods in your ND (non-dominant) hand with an overhand grip. (Using this hand may seem awkward at first, but you'll need your D (dominant) hand for manipulating the glass later.) Hold the rod at its balance point or center so that you'll be able to control the motion of the rod more easily. Turn it as continuously and smoothly as possible, rotating it toward or away from you. (The direction that you choose to use is a matter of personal preference. Either direction can seem awkward at first, so it may take a bit of time to sort out the one that gives you more control.)

Set your torch to a small, soft flame, and place the end of the glass rod in the flame. Turn it slowly enough to allow the heat to penetrate the glass and begin to soften (photo 1). Remember, it is the heat that does the work. (If you turn too quickly when you're trying to gathering a ball, it will actually take longer.)

2. If you see bubbles forming as you heat the cut end to molten, clean up the end of the rod before you go further. Below are two ways to do this that work well:

A. After you heat the end of the rod, take it out of the flame. Immediately use your tweezers to grab ONLY the molten glass (photo 2). Pull straight out so that a thin thread of glass emerges from the rod (photo 3). Stop pulling when the thread is about 3 to 4 inches (7.6-10.2 cm) long. Allow the thread to cool for a few seconds to harden, and put it back into the flame near the rod. The flame will *fire-cut* the thread.

B. Heat the rod, and pull a thread as you did in step A, but this time wrap the thread around the end of the rod, stopping when the thread hardens. Fire-cut the thread.

3. After you've cleaned the end of the rod, drop the the excess glass from your tweezers in your dropoff bucket. (If glass sticks to your tweezers, don't try to melt it off. Instead, hold the tweezers out of the flame until the glass hardens, or dip them in a small bowl of water. Then hit them against your work surface to break off the glass before you put it in your drop-off bucket.) Continue heating the end until it is nicely rounded (photo 4).

5

gravity

1. Hold the molten gather in the flame, and stop turning it (photo 6). The molten glass will immediately fall toward the workbench. To begin recentering the glass, rotate the rod halfway and allow the molten part to fall back toward the other side of the rod (photos 7 and 8).

You may have to start and stop several times to get the gather centered again. Sometimes all you need to do is begin rotating it evenly again once the gather is close to being centered, and allow gravity and atmospheric pressure to take over. As you do this, make sure that you're heating only the outer portion of the gather, i.e., the one farthest from the rod. If you place heat too close to the rod, you may lose control of the glass.

4. To continue making a gather, adjust your torch so that the flame is relatively hot and neutral to oxidizing. Once again, hold the rod of glass horizontally at its balance point with your ND hand in an overhand grip. Place the end of it in the flame, and rotate it slowly. As the glass becomes molten, move it into the flame a bit more until you see the end of the rod enlarge into a gather of molten glass (photo 5). (To tell if the ball is centered, run an imaginary line through the rod and the center of the ball.)

The size of the gather that you can create from a given diameter of rod depends on several things: how hot the flame is, how well you concentrate the heat on the glass, how well you keep the molten glass centered on the rod, and how you take advantage of gravity in the process.

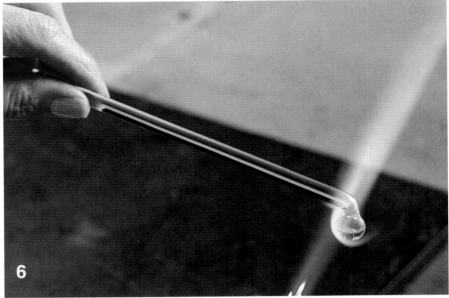
6

7

8

2. Hold the molten gather in the flame, LOWER the cut end of the rod down 6 to 10 inches (25.4 cm), and keep rotating the glass evenly (photo 9). You should notice the ball of glass flatten out into a mushroom-like shape. To bring it back into a round ball, resume a horizontal position with the rod, and keep rotating the glass in the flame.

3. Hold the molten gather in the flame, and RAISE the cut end of the rod up 6 to 10 (25.4 cm) inches (photo 10). As you rotate the glass evenly, the ball will stretch and elongate (photo 11). If you go too far with this process, the glass will get so thin that you'll lose control. Try it several times to learn where to stop. To bring the glass back, lower the cut end to a horizontal position or farther down, and keep rotating it until the glass becomes a round ball again.

fusing two rods

1. Clean up the polished end of each of the two rods that you'll be fusing together. (Round them in the flame, and use tweezers to remove any glass containing bubbles, as you did in step 2 of "Making a Gather of Glass".)

2. Set your torch to a relatively hot, sharp flame that is about ½ inch (1.3 cm) wide. Use an over-hand grip with your ND hand and either an overhand or underhand grip with your D hand. While rotating the rods, heat the polished end of each on opposite sides of the flame until they are white with heat (photo 12).

3. Remove them from the flame, and stick the two rods together (photo 13). If the glass is hot enough, it will flow together immediately.

4. Rotate the glass, and place the joined section back in the flame. Continue to rotate and heat it until the glass is fused together well. Push the two rods together to form a bulging, rounded place in the rod (photo 14).

5. Remove the fused rod from the flame, and continue to rotate it. Pull it slightly until the bulge disappears and is the about the same diameter as the rod (photo 15).

6. Position the fused rod on your graphite plate, and roll it back and forth until the glass is set up (photo 16). Doing this helps to even out the fused portion of the rod and make it straight.

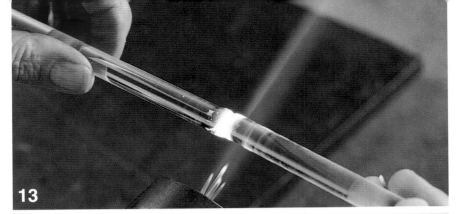

13

14

15

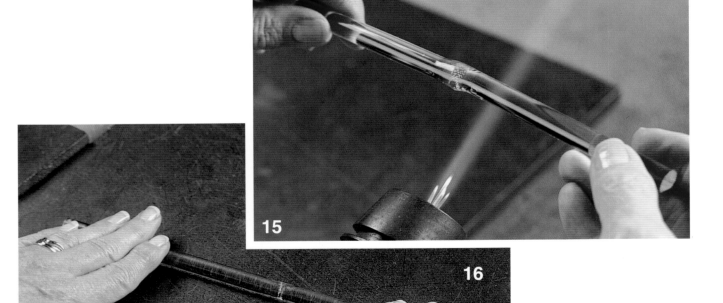

16

exercise 2—
MAKING A LEAF
AND VARIATIONS

In this exercise, you'll make a simple leaf shape and variations. This simple shape is one step toward preparing you to undertake more advanced methods of manipulating the glass to create more complicated shapes.

If you want to make leaves into functional things such as pendants, shade pulls, mobiles, or parts of a hanging sculpture, you'll need to add a loop at the base end of the leaf as the rod is removed. When you add this loop, keep in mind how you want the leaf to hang.

materials

Clear borosilicate rods:

6-10, 4 mm x 8 inches (20.3 cm) long

2, 7 mm x 12-15 inches (30.5-38.1 cm) long

2, 10 mm x 12-15 inches (30.5-38.1 cm) long

2, 12 mm x 12-15 inches (30.5-38.1 cm) long

tools

Parallel press/smasher or wide-bladed dinner knife

¼-inch (6 mm) graphite rod sharpened with pencil sharpener or small graphite reamer

Tweezers

leaf and variations

1. As you did in the previous exercise, gather a ball on the end of a 10 mm rod using a hot, neutral flame (photo 1).

2. Heat the ball to a very hot temperature. Take it out of the flame, and, with your ND hand, hold the cut end of the rod so that the rod is vertical. (By holding the glass rod in a vertical position, you're once again using gravity to your advantage to stretch the molten glass away from the solid rod. If you hold the rod in a horizontal position, the glass can sag down before you smash it, and you won't end up with a nice round disc.)

1

3. If you're using a parallel press/smasher, place it in your D hand before positioning the ball between the plates and pressing it together (photo 2). (This needs to be done fairly quickly, so the glass won't cool too much and begin to set up.) Make sure none of the solid rod gets between the plates of the smasher. If that happens, the solid glass will prevent the molten ball from flattening as much as it should. Remove the rod to reveal a disc (photo 3).

If you're using a dinner knife instead of a smasher, place the ball on the graphite plate, and flatten it with the knife.

4. Next, you'll learn how to fire-polish the surface of the glass to remove surface imperfections. (Anytime you touch the molten glass with a metal tool—such as the smasher or the knife—the sudden cooling that occurs results in imperfections.) To fire-polish the disc, hold the rod horizontally and brush half of one side of it through the flame until the marks are gone (photo 4). Turn the disc over and do the same to the reverse half. Then polish the other half of both sides of the disc. (Working on half of the disc at a time keeps the glass from flopping around on the end of the rod.)

5. For this step, change your torch to a small, fine-pointed flame. If you practice the following method several times, you'll be able to gauge how small and hot the flame needs to be.

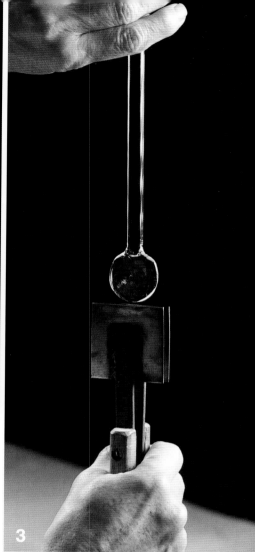

You'll begin by attaching a punty made from a 4 mm rod to the other edge of the disc at a point directly in line with the 10 mm rod. (A punty is a temporary handle that holds the glass while you manipulate it into a shape. You may need to attach and detach a punty several times during the process of making an object.)

To attach a punty, continuously rotate the 10 mm rod with the disc attached as you do the following: Hold the 4 mm rod in your D hand with an underhand grip. Using each side of the flame, simultaneously heat the

4

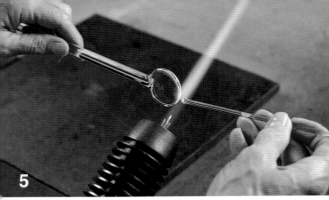

5

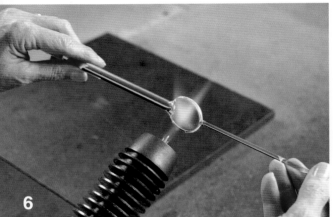

6

7

8

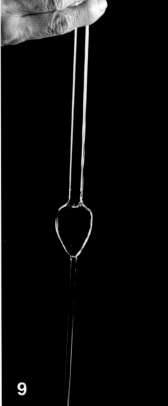

9

flame. Hold the rod vertically with the cut end up, and gently pull on the punty to stretch the disc slightly in the center (photo 7). (Don't pull too hard, or you'll end up with an hourglass shape.)

8. Repeat the previous step with one modification: This time, heat the disc closer to the edge where the punty is attached (photo 8). (Be careful not to overheat the piece, or heat it too close to the punty, because you might pull the punty off when you pull the disc. If that happens, simply reattach the punty.) Once the glass is softened, take it out of the flame before holding and pulling it into a more pointed end that forms the tip of the leaf (photo 9).

end of the 4 mm rod and the spot on the disc where you need to attach it (photo 5). When they both reach the same red-hot stage, take them out of the flame and stick them together, aligning the punty with the 10 mm rod. Continue to rotate the rods as they set up to keep them in line.

6. Now you're ready to pull the disc into a leaf shape. Hold the 10 mm rod in your ND hand with an overhand grip while you hold the punty in your D hand with an underhand grip. With the same small flame, heat the center of the disc on each side, flipping it from one side to the other (photo 6). (Don't waste your time heating the edges of the disc.)

7. When the disc is glowing red and pliable, remove it from the

10

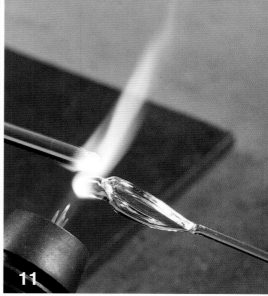

11

9. To remove the leaf from the rod, heat it with a strong, hot flame about ½ inch (1.3 cm) wide. Hold the rod in your ND hand with an overhand grip and the punty in your D hand with an underhand grip. Rotate the rod while you hold it in the flame about ¼ inch (6 mm) from the base of the leaf (photo 10). When the glass is hot enough, take it out of the flame and pull the leaf away to form a thin thread of glass. Fire-cut the thread near the leaf by allowing the thread to cool to solid before placing it back in the flame and cutting it (photo 11).

10. Next you need to form a slight ball at the base of the leaf. Hold the punty with your D hand, and gently heat the rod at the base of the leaf until the bit of thread is absorbed and a ball is formed (photo 12). The ball should be large enough that it fuses well and can hold the weight of the leaf later.

Clean up the end of the rod from which you removed the leaf by heating the thread in the flame until it is absorbed back into the end of the rod. (Always take time to fire-polish and round up the ends of rods once you have finished making an object. If you leave a thread attached to the end of a rod, it may end up sticking you.) Place the leaf with punty attached into your wooden block.

11. Perform these steps several times until you can make a fairly well shaped leaf, and experiment with different sized rods. (The size of the leaf that you make will vary with the diameter of the rods you use.)

12. The leaves that you've made with the process above are flat and stylized. You can use them as they are or make them appear more natural by twisting or bending them as described on page 50.

12

twisting the leaf

1. Make a basic leaf, but stop before removing the rod or punty. Hold the rod in your ND hand with an overhand grip and the punty in your D hand with an underhand grip. Gently heat the center portion of the leaf with a soft, medium-sized flame (photo 13).

2. As the glass softens, begin to rotate the rod. In your D hand, turn the punty at a slightly slower rate than the rod so that it drags a bit. You'll see the leaf begin to twist. Keep this up until the leaf is as twisted as you'd like it to be (photo 14). However, don't twist it so much that creases form in the glass, because these creases are cracks waiting to happen. (Remember, a crease is any sharp indentation in the surface of the glass. If you have trouble seeing creases, rub the blade of a knife or the tip of a tungsten pick over the surface of the glass. Any place that either tool catches is a crease. You can also do this with your fingernail after the glass has cooled completely.)

3. Hold the leaf out of the flame and perfectly still for a few seconds until the glass sets up (photo 15). You'll know that this has happened when the glass looks clear again and it doesn't move. Remove the leaf from the rod as described on page 49. Save the leaf with a punty attached to the tip for a later project, or attach a loop by following the steps on page 51.

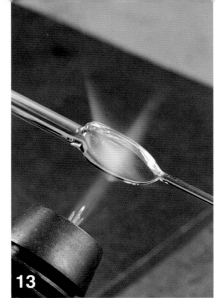

13

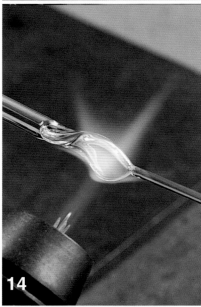

14

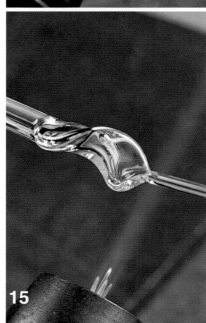

15

bending the leaf

1. Follow step 1 under "twisting the leaf."

2. Heat the center of the leaf until the glass is soft enough that it begins to move easily (photo 16). Now you can bend the leaf in any direction you wish (photo 17).

3. Move the glass quickly, take it out of the flame, and hold it perfectly still until the glass has set up (photo 18). Fire-polish any creases or surface imperfections that may have resulted from bending the glass.

4. Save the leaf with a punty attached to the tip for a later project, or attach a loop as described next.

16

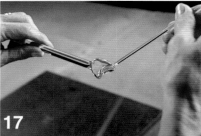

17

18

adding a finishing loop

1. Make a leaf and leave the rod and punty attached. Adjust your torch so that it has a soft, hot flame. Place the punty in your ND hand with an overhand grip and the rod in your D hand with an underhand grip. Rotate the rod in the flame, heating it about ¼ inch (6 mm) from the base of the leaf.

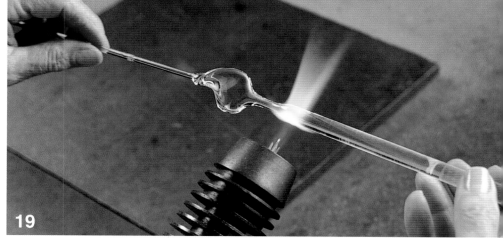

2. When the glass is pliable, begin to pull gently. At the same time, continue to heat the rod just ahead of where the glass is moving as you pull (photo 19). Continue doing this until you've pulled a tapered length of glass (a tail) that is about 1 inch (2.5 cm) long. (To prevent overheating the glass, so that it pulls off too quickly, you can dip the glass in and out of the flame to slow down the heat.)

3. Remove the rod by cutting the glass in the flame (photo 20).

4. Adjust your torch to a small, soft flame. Hold the punty horizontally with the tail just above the flame. Don't rotate the glass. Begin to heat the tail from the end toward the leaf, allowing the glass to fall and curl downward (photo 21). When the tail has curved about halfway back toward the leaf, take your tweezers in your D hand, grab the end of the tail, and bend it around until it is touching the leaf (photo 22).

5. Heat the glass until both areas are well fused with no crease where they touch (photo 23). You won't have a perfect loop at this point.

6. Increase the heat of the torch a bit, and aim the flame right up through the hole that has been created. The glass will begin to shrink. (You may have to bob the loop in and out of the flame as a way of controlling how quickly the loop shrinks.) Using the sharpened graphite rod or small graphite reamer in your D hand, stick the pointed end into the hole of the loop, and rotate it back and forth until you have a nice round hole in the loop (photo 24).

7. Hold the leaf with your tweezers in your ND hand. Heat the attachment point of the punty, and pull it away with your D hand (photo 25). Fire-polish the punty's point, and shape the tip of the leaf (photo 26).

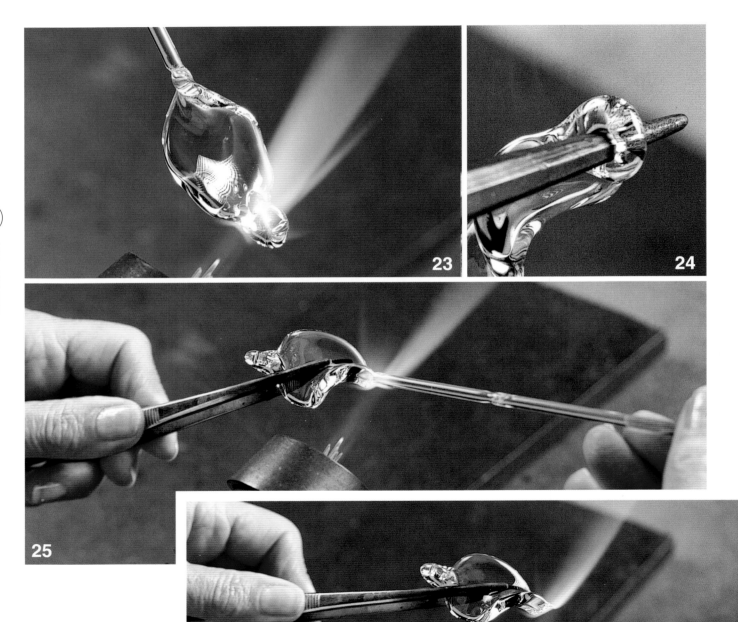

exercise 3—
EMBELLISHING
LEAVES

In this exercise, you'll learn several ways to embellish the surface and the edges of leaves. Then you'll learn the next most important thing that you need to know when working with borosilicate glass: how to fuse two pieces of glass together properly. (No matter how wonderful your glass shapes are, if you can't properly fuse two pieces of glass together, everything you make will eventually fall apart.)

Rather than gathering a ball of molten glass at the end of a rod as you did in exercise 1, you'll begin this part of the exercise by making a ball in the middle of a rod, allowing you to make a ball almost double the size of the other one. Then you'll add lines to simulate leaf veins. You'll also learn four ways to embellish the edges of leaves in different and interesting ways.

materials

Clear borosilicate rods:

6-10, 4 mm x 8 inches (20. 3 cm) long

2, 7 mm x 12–15 inches (30.5-38.1 cm) long

2, 10 mm x 12–15 inches (30.5-38.1 cm) long

2, 12 mm x 12–15 inches (30.5-38.1 cm) long

tools

Parallel press/smasher

Wide-bladed dinner knife

Tweezers

Glass-cutting scissors

Graphite plate

Wooden block with holes

leaf with vein lines

1. Select a 10 mm rod that is 15 inches (38.1 cm) or slightly longer. Use an overhand grip to hold it with your ND hand at one end and an underhand grip to hold it at the other end with your D hand. Set your torch at a hot and neutral to oxidizing flame that is about ½ inch (1.3 cm) wide.

2. Place the center of the rod in the flame with one hand on either side of the area that you're heating (photo 1). Rotate it evenly and begin to heat the rod to molten so that it begins to form a ball (photo 2). If this setting is not hot enough, adjust your torch to a larger, hotter flame. (You can use an overhand grip with your D hand as well for this part until you've made and centered the molten ball. Then switch back to an underhand grip.)

1

4. When you've gathered as much glass as you want, remove the end of the rod in your D hand by heating it in the flame and pulling it off (photo 4). Continue heating the molten ball, remove it from the flame (photo 5), and smash it as you did in exercise 2 (see page 47). Fire-polish the resulting disc.

5. Change your flame to a hot, narrow one to prepare for making the center vein of the leaf. On one side of the disc, heat it right down the center beginning where the rod connects and moving to the opposite edge of the disc. Move back and forth through the flame until the surface of the disc is softened.

6. Pick up the knife with your D hand. Take the disc out of the flame and immediately place it

2

3

4

3. As the rod softens, work first on one side of the gather and then the other, incorporating the rod into the molten glass from each side (photo 3). As you do this, the ends of the rod you're using as handles will shorten on both sides. (If they get too short, you'll have to limit the size of the ball you make. Do this exercise several times to learn which length rod works best for you.)

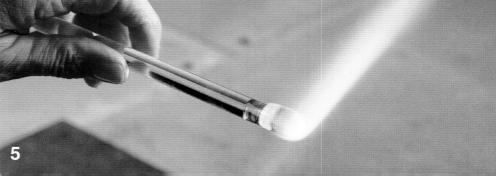

5

on a graphite plate with the soft-ened side of the glass up (you can use the graphite of your large paddle for this). Press into the center of the softened glass with the knife and lift up quickly, leaving a mark in the glass that looks like the main vein of the leaf (photo 6).

7. To create side veins, heat half of the disc on one side of the center vein (you may need to adjust your flame to a slightly larger, bushier flame). When the glass has softened, place the disc on the graphite, and use the knife to press a series of lines that run diagonally to the center line (photo 7).

8. Repeat this step with the other half of the disc (photo 8).

9. Opposite the rod, attach a punty to the other side of the disc along the center line.

10. Change your flame to a small, pointed one. To finish the process, heat the BLANK side of the disc in the center to move the glass around in a small circle. Slightly fuse and relax any sharp creases left by the knife. On the veined side, occasionally brush the surface with heat, being careful to avoid fusing the vein lines com-pletely back together (photo 9).

11. When the glass has softened, gently pull the disc into a leaf shape using the steps outlined in exercise 2 (photo 10). Leave the punty attached, and place it in your wooden block to cool.

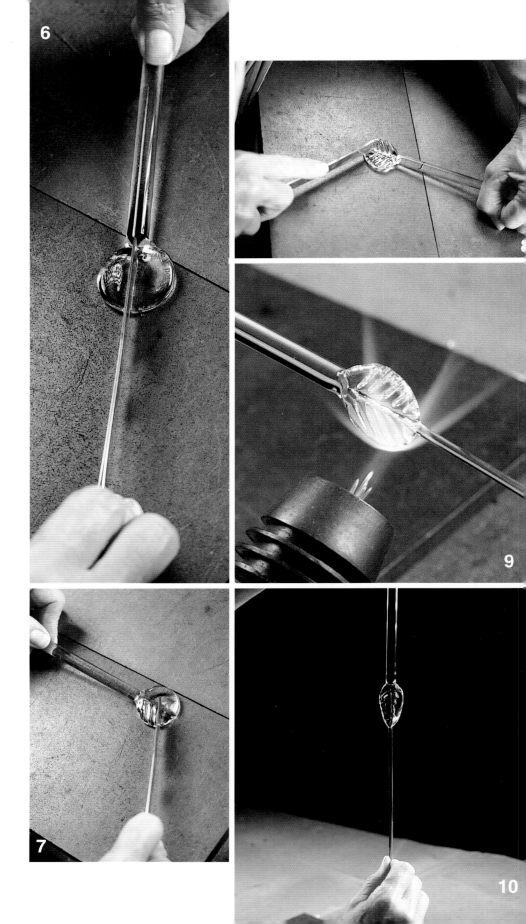

leaf with edge work

1. Make another simple leaf shape, gathering the ball of molten glass either at the end of the rod or in the center. Remove the punty.

2. To embellish the edges of the leaf, use one of the following methods. For all three variations, begin by holding the rod in your ND hand with the leaf toward the flame, then adjust your flame until it is small and hot (photo 11).

Crimped effect: Pick up your tweezers in your D hand. Heat a small section of the edge of the leaf near the rod. Take it out of the flame, and repeatedly squeeze the softened glass with the tweezers several times along the edge to create small indentations (photo 12). (If the tweezers become overheated and begin sticking, dip them in a small fireproof container of water to cool them off as you work.) Heat the adjacent section of the edge and add another series of marks until you reach the tip of the leaf (photo 13). Repeat this process on the other side of the leaf, beginning at the rod end. Attach a punty to the free end, and remove the leaf from the rod. Store the piece in your wooden block.

11

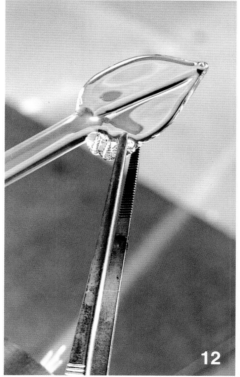

12

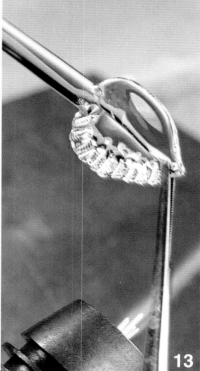

13

Ruffled effect: With the tweezers in your D hand, heat a small section of the edge of the leaf near the rod. When the glass has softened, take the leaf out of the flame and grab the softened glass along the heated edge with the tweezers, twisting it at a 90° angle and pulling it slightly (photo 14). Repeat this process along the edge of the leaf until you reach the tip, leaving small gaps between each twist of the glass (photo 15). Repeat on the other side, moving from the rod to the tip. Attach a punty, and remove the leaf from the rod (photo 16). Store the piece in your wooden block.

Spiked effect: This method of creating an edge is slightly more difficult than the previous ones and may take more practice. Aim the flame slightly inside the edge of the leaf in a small area near the rod (instead of directly on the edge as you did before). When the area has softened, take a punty in your D hand, and touch the edge of the glass before pulling a bit of the glass quickly into a point or spike. Begin to

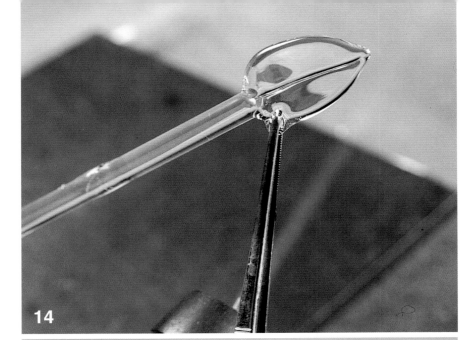

14

15

16

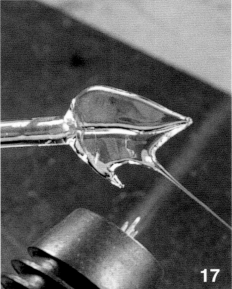

17

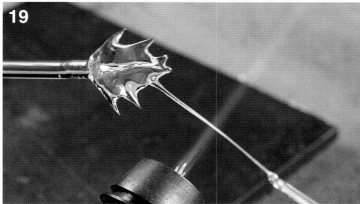

pull spikes along the edge of the leaf, leaving gaps between them (photo 17). Work from the bottom of the leaf to the top so that the heat won't melt the sections you've just completed (photos 18 and 19). Attach a punty to the tip, and remove the leaf from the rod (photo 20).

Diagonally cut edge: About a third to half of the way up the leaf toward its tip, heat a small line in the glass that runs from the edge at a diagonal toward the center. Move the leaf back and forth along this line in the flame until it is softened (photo 21). (If needed, flip the leaf over and follow the line on the other side to make sure the glass is evenly softened all the way through.)

With scissors in your D hand, cut into the softened glass at a diagonal (photo 22). Turn the leaf over and repeat this process on the other side, mirroring the line that you've already cut (photo 23).

Before proceeding, you need to fire-polish the cuts where they end in solid glass. (If you don't do this where the sharp creases have been formed, the glass will end up cracking.) Use a small flame to heat the glass at the end of the cut line until it softens and rounds out (photo 24). Use the flame to attach a punty to the top of the leaf (the largest, upper-most section). Heat the section until it is soft (photo 25). Remove it from the flame and pull gently, curving the glass slightly (photo 26). Repeat this process by adding punties and pulling on the remaining two (lower) sections of the leaf at the tips (photos 27 and 28). Remove the leaf from the rod (photo 29). Place it in your wooden block.

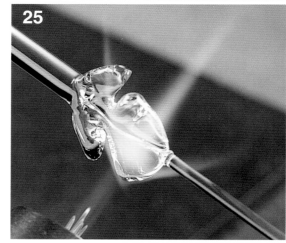

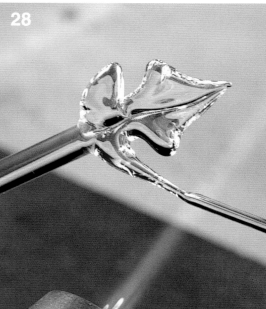

exercise 4—
MAKING MARIAS AND
TRANSITIONAL SHAPES

In this exercise, you'll make what are known as "marias" and other transitional shapes (such as round ball shapes) from a clear glass rod. Marias are disc-like shapes that are formed by compressing the length of a glass rod. They can be used between glass components that you want to assemble together in a straight line. They're often used to make parts such as candlestick stems or wine glass stems. You can create a beautiful piece using nothing but a continuous lines of these shapes on a clear rod.

materials

Clear borosilicate glass rods:

2,10 mm x 12-15 inches (30.5-38.1 cm) long

tools

Graphite reamer (optional)

instructions

1. Hold a 10 mm clear rod in an underhand position in your D hand and an overhand position in your ND hand. Adjust the flame on your torch to a narrow, sharp-edged flame that isn't too hot. At a point on the rod about 2 inches (5.1 cm) from your ND hand, begin to rotate the glass in the flame. Turn the glass as evenly as possible, so that the heat soaks the rod throughout (photo 1).

2. Heat the glass until it is soft and molten, but not white. When it is soft enough, remove the rod from the flame, and gently push together from either end with both hands, causing the glass to begin to bulge out (photo 2).

3. Don't expect the disc to form with a single push. The rhythm to use is "push-turn-push-turn-push-turn." Rotate the rod a quarter of the way around with each turn. Keep pushing and turning until the glass sets up, or until the maria is a shape that you like (photo 3).

(Keep in mind that marias must be made in one continous movement—you can't reheat the glass and change them. It takes practice to make them evenly shaped. To assist this process: Don't make the glass too soft, don't push too hard [especially the first time], keep your hands perfectly aligned, and keep the glass rotating all the time.)

4. Once you've mastered making a maria, try making three in a row. Heat an area toward your D hand about ½ inch (1.3 cm) from the first one (photo 4), and make a second one (photo 5). Repeat this process to make the third one (photos 6 and 7).

5. Now you're ready to make a series of transitional shapes. Work out a pattern of shapes in your mind, and give it a try using 10 mm glass. For instance, you can make a pattern such as three marias, a ball, a maria, a ball, and three marias (photo 8). (How to form a ball is explained on page 40.)

The fun part about making these sections of rod with transitional shapes is that you can plan the shapes in advance or intuitively add them as you go along.

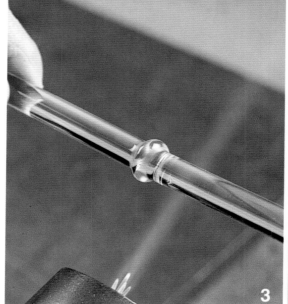

6. To make your sample shapes into something functional, pull one end of the rod to a point as you remove it from the flame. Attach a punty. Use a graphite reamer to form a loop on the other end of the rod as you remove it (see pages 51 and 52 for more information about loops). Remove the punty, and you've made a hanging glass "drop."

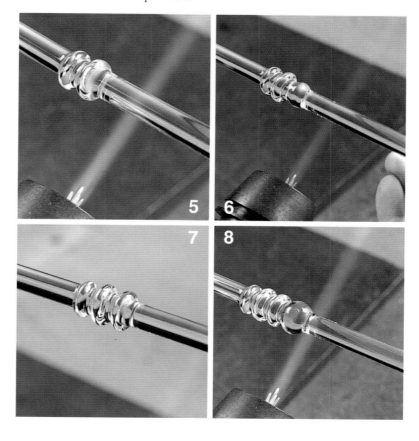

exercise 5—
CASING A CLEAR
ROD WITH COLOR

In this exercise you'll learn to stripe colored glass on a clear glass rod, a technique that makes your colored glass go a lot further. This technique of completely coating the clear rod with color is called "casing the rod." You can cover clear glass with colored or colored glass with clear. In this exercise, you'll cover a clear rod.

materials

Clear borosilicate rods:

1-2, 10 mm x 8 inches (20.3 cm) long

1, 12 mm x 12 inches (30.5 cm) long

1 ruby-colored glass rod

tools

Tweezers

Wooden block with holes in it

instructions

1. Clean up the end of a 12 mm rod, and warm 3 inches (7.6 cm) of it at the end of the flame (photo 1). (Use a soft, relatively hot flame that isn't too wide.)

2. Hold a clear rod in your ND hand, and position it just below the flame. Hold the tip of the colored rod in the flame so that it melts just enough to flow. Beginning at a point about 3 inches (7.6 cm) from the end of

the clear rod, you'll begin to apply the colored stripe. Applying color correctly requires doing several new things at once: First, touch the tip of the colored rod to the warmed, clear glass. Then immediately bend the colored rod away from the flame to expose the maximum amount of the colored rod to the flame. Aim the flame right at the bottom of the colored rod where it touches the clear rod.

At the same time, gradually move the clear rod UP while you SLOWLY rotate the colored rod, and press it into the clear glass (photo 2). By doing this, you will keep the colored rod in the flame so that the glass is molten enough to flow onto the clear rod. Rotating the colored rod slowly allows constant exposure of cooler glass to the flame. (If you fail to do this, one side of the colored rod will be nice and hot and the other side will be cool, keeping the color from flowing smoothly.) Continue laying the color to the end of the rod (photo 3).

3. Fuse the colored stripe that you've created onto the clear glass before proceeding. To do this, begin at the tip of the rod and work backwards, heating only the area where the color touches the clear. You'll see the two glasses flow together if you're doing this correctly. If cracking occurs, heal the cracks by heating them until the glass fuses together and they're gone (photo 4).

4. Lay on a second colored stripe right next to the first one so that there is no space between the two stripes of color, overlapping the color slightly if you wish (photo 5). Orient your glass rod in the flame as you did before.

5. Continue to lay on color until the entire clear rod is covered with stripes, and there is no clear glass showing between them (photo 6).

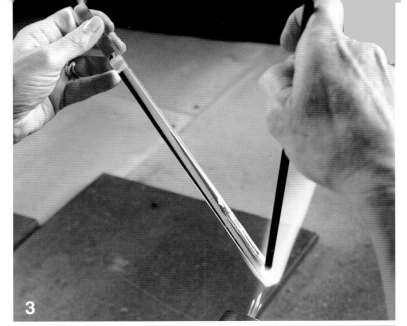

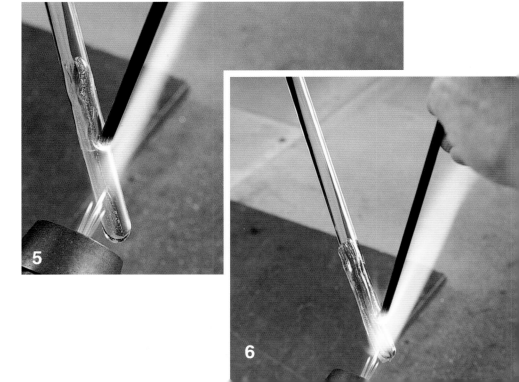

6. Attach a 10 mm rod to the end of the clear rod that you've just covered. Make sure that it is well fused to the 12 mm rod as well as centered and straight. Hold the 10 mm rod with your D hand.

7. Beginning on the end where the 10 mm rod is attached to the base of the striped rod, slowly rotate the rod in the flame, fusing all of the colored glass to the clear rod. You should see any creases that may have formed between the colored stripes disappear as the colored stripes are fused (photo 7).

8. Continually rotate the rod, and gradually move toward the other end with the flame. You need to work all the way from one end of the rod to the other so that any air trapped in the small tunnels between the colored stripes is pushed out the open end (photo 8).

9. Once you've fused all of the colored glass, pull the rod to a diameter of 10 mm. To do this, begin at the end that has the 10 mm rod attached, and heat the glass again while rotating until it is soft enough to pull slightly so that it is elongated. Pull the section you're working on so that the diameter is close to that of the attached rod.

10. Move slowly up the rod, heating it while continuing to pull with your D hand. Continue this process until you have reached the other end of the stripes, and the colored rod is elongated into a 10 mm rod (photo 9).

11. Leave the clear 10 mm rod attached, and remove the colored rod from the original 12 mm rod (photo 10). Remove any clear glass still attached to that end with your tweezers.

12. Set the new colored rod aside to cool, or, if you like, anneal it first before allowing it to cool.

7

8

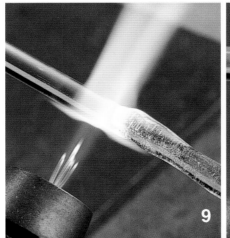

9

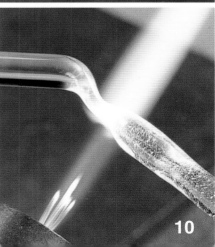

10

exercise 6—
MAKING A HEART SHAPE

To make a heart, you'll begin by casing a clear rod with ruby glass as you did in exercise 5. To get the feel of making the heart, try making it in clear glass before you add color.

materials

Clear borosilicate rods:

6-10, 4 mm x 8 inches (20.3 cm) long

2, 10 mm x 8 inches (20.3 cm) long

2, 12 mm x 12 inches (30.5 cm) long

1 ruby-colored glass rod

tools

Wide-bladed dinner knife

Tweezers

Parallel press/smasher

Wooden block with holes

instructions

1. Case a 12 mm clear rod with ruby-colored glass using the 10 mm rod as a handle as you did in exercise 5. Gather a ball at the end of the rod (photo 1). (As you do this, the ruby-colored glass will become clear in the molten state, but there will be a noticeable difference between the density of it and the clear glass. You'll notice that the top of the ball has less colored glass than the bottom that is still attached to the rod—especially if you hold the cut end of the turning rod down as you gather the ball. As you hold the end of the rod down while heating it to form a ball, the outside skin of the glass will slide down toward the base of the ball. At the same time, the center of the molten rod will move up toward the top of the ball. This also happens when you're heating a clear rod, but you can't see what's going on. The color makes it more apparent.) You can use this phenomenon to create various graduated colors on molten balls. If you don't want the color to range from dark to almost clear, add more color to the top of the ball.)

2. Hold the rod vertically, and smash the ball into a flat disc (photo 2).

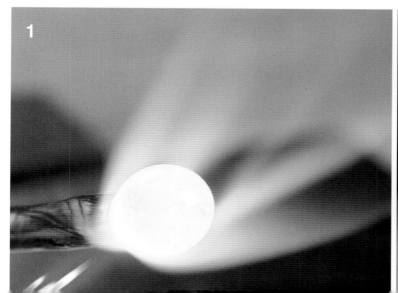

3. Attach a 4 mm punty to the disc opposite and in line with the 10 mm rod.

4. Heat the center of the disc. To form the bottom point of the heart, pull the disc as if you were making a leaf (photo 3), but don't pull it into quite as long a point (photo 4). Leave the punty attached, and hold it with your D hand.

5. With your flame narrow and hot, begin to heat the disc where the rod is attached, rather than heating the rod itself (photo 5). As the glass softens, flip the disc from one flat side to the other, and begin to pull gently.

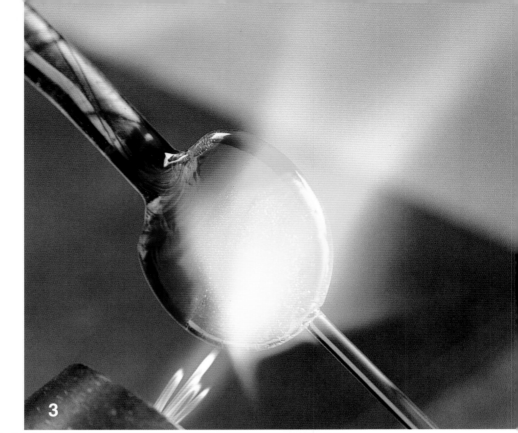

3

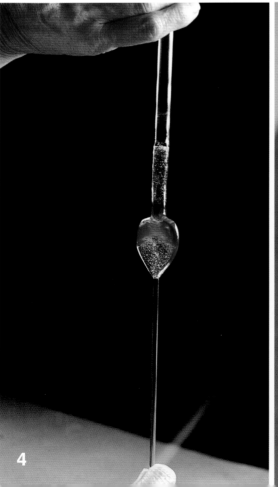

4

5

6. As you pull the rod away (photo 6), pull out a small portion of the disc (photo 7). Continue to heat that spot while holding the point of the heart down. The glass should retract and form an indentation on the edge of the disc opposite the point.

7. Heat the indentation until it is molten. Take it out of the flame, and hold it vertically. Press your knife into it with a rolling action to form a cleft at the top of the heart (photo 8). If a crease forms, fire-polish it away.

8. Use a small, hot flame to continue heating the heart, allowing gravity to move the glass around the edges as you form a nice heart shape (photos 9 and 10). If you need to remove excess glass during the shaping process, use your tweezers, or use the tip of a cold rod to touch and pull the excess molten glass away.

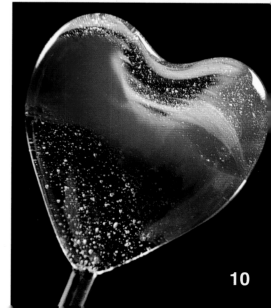

exercise 7—
MAKING A FISH SHAPE
WITH FRIT COLOR

In this exercise, you'll use colored glass frit and clear rod to create a fish shape. Then you'll use a colored rod to "wipe on" glass for the fins and tail. (To learn the technique, you may want to try this exercise using clear glass without color before adding it.)

Frit is made up of crushed glass. Keep in mind that breathing glass dust from powdered frit can be very dangerous to your health, so always take precautions. Wear a mask, and take care not to stir up the dust as you use the frit. Don't use it in an area with a draft. After you're finished, clean it up with dampened cloth.

materials

Clear borosilicate rods:

6-10, 4 mm x 8 inches (20.3 cm) long

2, 10 mm x 8 inches (20.3 cm) long

1, 12 mm x 12 inches (30.5 cm) long

Colored frit in one or two colors of your choice

Several 7 mm colored glass rods of your choice

tools

Graphite plate

Parallel press/smasher

Wide-bladed dinner knife (optional)

¼-inch (6 mm) graphite rod with flat end

Wooden block with holes in it

instructions

1. First, select the color(s) of frit that you want to use—one, several different, or a mixture. Use a small spoon to carefully scoop the frit out of its container, or gently pour some onto the graphite plate (photo 1). (Be careful not to create a cloud of glass dust that you might inhale.) Use your finger or a wide-bladed knife to spread the frit out in a uniform layer.

2. Make a ball on the end of a clear 12 mm glass rod, and smash it into a disc with the smasher.

1

3. Heat the disc until it's very soft, and press the flat side into the frit (photo 2). If it's hot enough, some of the frit will stick to the disc. Immediately place the disc back into the flame, and heat the bits of frit until they fuse into the clear glass (photo 3). You can repeat this process several times, incorporating other colors as you wish (photo 4). As you pick up the frit, use your smasher as needed to adjust the disc shape between steps.

4. Attach a 4 mm punty to the side of the disc opposite the turning rod (photo 5). Heat and pull a small point as you did when you made a heart in the previous exercise (photo 6). Remove the punty. This will be the body of the fish.

5. Choose a rod in a color of your choice to make into the fins.

6. Hold the turning rod in your ND hand while heating one edge of the fish body. Use a narrow, relatively hot flame. (The placement of the glass in this technique is much like that of casing a rod.) Place the fish body underneath the flame, just touching the edge of the glass while placing the tip of the colored rod in the flame.

7. Heat the end of the colored rod, and touch it to the back of the fish toward the end where the turning rod is attached. Lay a stripe of color on the edge of the glass by moving the fish body

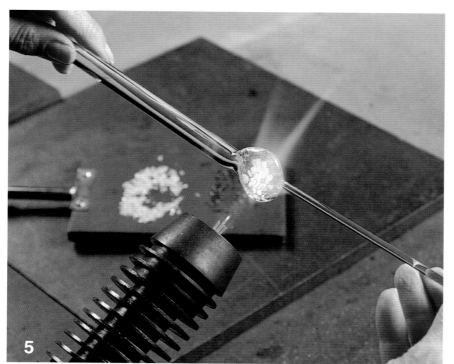

forward, keeping the colored rod in the same spot in the flame (photo 7).

8. Without removing the colored rod from the flame, lift and turn it as you return the fish to its original position. Once again, use the rod to touch the first stripe of color where it begins, and lay another stripe of color on top of the first.

9. Repeat the previous step as many times as you like while you build up a fin with subsequent stripes of color on top of one another (photo 8). This technique takes some practice to develop a rhythm that allows the colored glass to stay soft as you lift, turn, and lay it on without becoming so soft that you lose control.

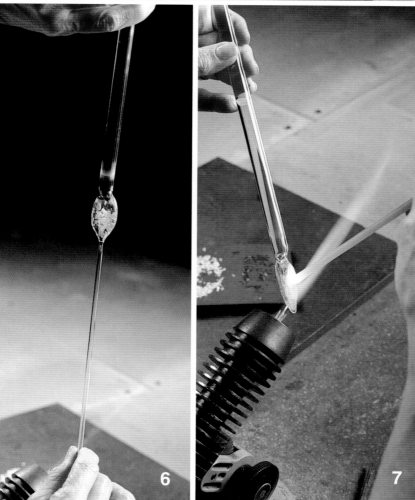

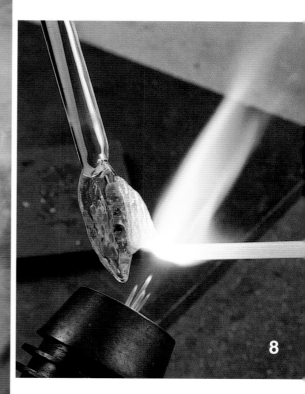

10. When you have added enough layers, pull on the colored rod at the end of a stripe to form a thread, and fire-cut it to remove the colored rod. Heat and shape the fin as you pull the colored rod away.

11. Fuse the ends of the first stripe at the front and back where it touches the body of the fish. Then make sure that the entire first stripe is well fused to the body (photo 9).

12. Heat the whole fin so that any creases between stripes are fused.

13. Attach a punty to the tip of the fin. Heat the fin, then pull and stretch it again to a shape that you want. If you fused the color well and do this step correctly, you'll still retain definition between the individual stripes. Remove the punty.

14. Use the same process to create an abdominal fin (photo 10) and two tail fins (photo 11). Make sure to fuse the V-shaped point where the two tail fins touch each other as well as where the fins touch the fish body.

15. To make eyes for the fish, begin by using a very narrow, hot flame to heat a spot for placing one of the eyes. Heat the tip of a dark colored rod, and fuse on a spot of color to form the eye (photos 12 and 13).

16. Remove the fish from the flame, and lay the head of it on a graphite plate with the eye facing

9

10

11

12

13

you. Press into the eye with the flat end of a ¼-inch (6 mm) graphite rod (photo 14).

17. Repeat the previous two steps to add an eye on the other side of the head.

18. Attach a punty to the tip of one of the tail fins. Make sure that the punty is parallel to the turning rod (even though it probably won't be in line with it). Heat the turning rod where it is attached to the fish body, and remove it along with any clear glass that remains (photos 15 and 16). This is the area where you'll place the mouth. Switch the punty to your ND hand.

19. With your D hand, heat the end of a colored rod to make a small ball. On opposite sides of the same flame, heat the colored ball and the spot on the fish where the mouth will be. Attach the ball to the fish and fuse it (photo 17).

20. Continue to heat the colored ball until it is very soft. Then take the fish out of the flame, and hold the body vertically with the mouth down.

21. Press into the soft colored ball with the side of your ¼-inch (6 mm) graphite rod to create the mouth and lips of the fish (photos 18 and 19).

22. If you plan to incorporate this fish into something such as a candlestick stem, go ahead and add clear glass attachment points while the fish is still hot. To do

this, heat a 7 or 10 mm rod, and place a small ball of glass at each point where it will join another piece.

23. Place the piece in your wooden block for assembly with another piece later, or remove the punty if you don't plan to do this.

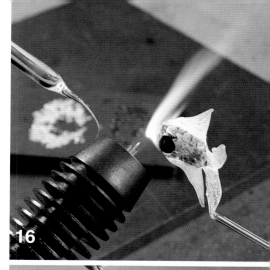

16

17

14

15

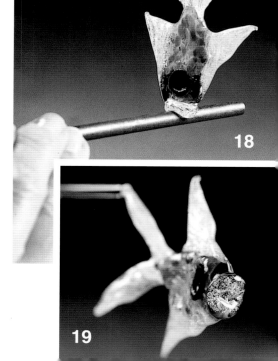

18

19

exercise 8—
MAKING A FLOWER

*I*n this exercise, you'll create a daisy-like flower with five petals from clear glass. When you make a flower, you'll learn to make and use "bridges." You're now making an object that is complex enough that you must calculate the best order for making and assembling the parts. Although the steps are shown to you in this exercise, practicing it will move you through the process and lend you experience for building other pieces.

materials

Clear borosilicate rods:

6-10, 4 mm x 8 inches (20.3 cm) long

2 or 3, 7 mm x 15 inches (38.1 cm) long

2, 10 mm x 15 inches (38.1 cm) long

tools

Wide-bladed dinner knife

Tweezers

Graphite plate

Parallel press/smasher

Tungsten tool, pick, or paring knife (optional)

instructions

1. To make five petals from the 7 mm rods, use the same technique that you used in exercise 2 to make a leaf with a center vein (see page 54). Try to make all of the petals approximately the same size. (You may have to make more than five and then pick the ones that come closest to each other in size.) Leave the punties attached to the petals.

2. Gather a ball of glass at the end of the 10 mm rod. Once you've made the ball, take it out of the flame, and keep rotating it so that it becomes solid (photos 1 and 2).

3. To create the top center section of the flower, heat the top of the ball, and flatten it on your piece of graphite (photo 3).

4. To work out the spacing for the petals, heat a small amount of glass at the end of a 7 mm rod before heating a spot along the edge of the flattened flower center. Fuse the heated glass at the end of the rod to that spot on the edge. (Heat both the spot and the rod at the same time on opposite sides of the flame.) Continue heating until the glass you've added is well fused and a raised spot results. (You'll attach one of your petals to this spot.)

5. Continue around the edge of the center with the same procedure until you have five evenly spaced spots for attaching petals around the flower center (photo 4).

6. Now you're ready to attach the petals. Hold one petal at a time by the punty in your D hand. On opposite sides of the flame at the same time, heat the attachment point on the base of the petal and a spot on the edge where it will be attached. When both areas have reached a white-hot state, remove them from the flame and push them together until they touch (photo 5). (If the glass is hot enough, you should see the molten glass flow together. If it is not quite hot enough, you will get a crease where the two glasses have been pushed together. Use this for future reference, and move on.) Remove the punty (photo 6) and set it aside.

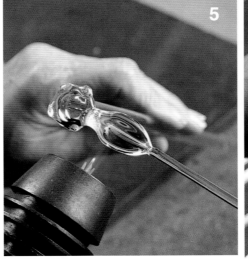

7. Continue adding the rest of the petals in the same way as quickly as possible (photos 7 and 8).

8. Next, fuse the joints between the petals and the flower's center together to get rid of creases. Reattach one of the 4 mm punties you removed in step 6 to the tip of one of the petals to form a temporary bridge for holding

everything in place as you fuse (photo 9). (If you don't take this step, the petals won't stay in place.)

9. Heat and bend the punty around so that it touches the tip of the next petal, and fuse it there (photo 10). Bend it around until it touches the next tip and fuse it again, continuing this process until you have connected all of

the petal tips (photo 11). If your punty isn't long enough to go around the flower, simply fuse another one onto the one you're using and keep going.

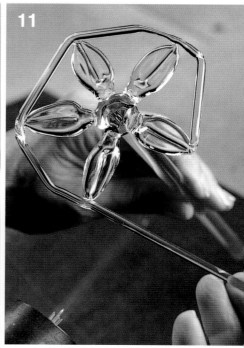

10. At the points where you attached the petals, use a small, hot flame to heat each joint until it is well fused, applying the flame from both the front and the back (photos 12 and 13). Work your way around the petals to fuse all of the joints in this manner.

(If one of the bridge attachments breaks and the petal starts moving around, hold the petal in the correct position with your tweezers until the glass is solid again. Reattach the tip to the bridge and continue fusing.)

11. If you wish, you can texturize the center of the flower by heating it and poking it with the tungsten tool, pick, or the end of your paring knife (photo 14).

12. To remove the bridges, heat the 4 mm rods between each of the petals (photo 15). Pull away a small section of each to leave a gap in the bridge between each petal (photos 16).

13. Heat the tip of each petal, and pull away the excess 4 mm rod using your tweezers (photo 17).

14. Attach a 7 mm punty to the tip of one of the petals, parallel to the rod that holds the flower, and fuse it well (photo 18). (You're using a thicker punty because it will need to hold the entire weight of the flower.)

15. Remove the entire flower from the 10 mm rod about ½ inch (1.3 cm) down from the center of the flower (photo 19). Gather the glass back in the flame so that there's a nice-sized ball for attaching the flower to a stem later on (photo 20).

16. You can anneal the flower at this stage, if you wish.

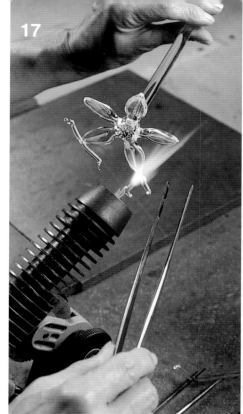

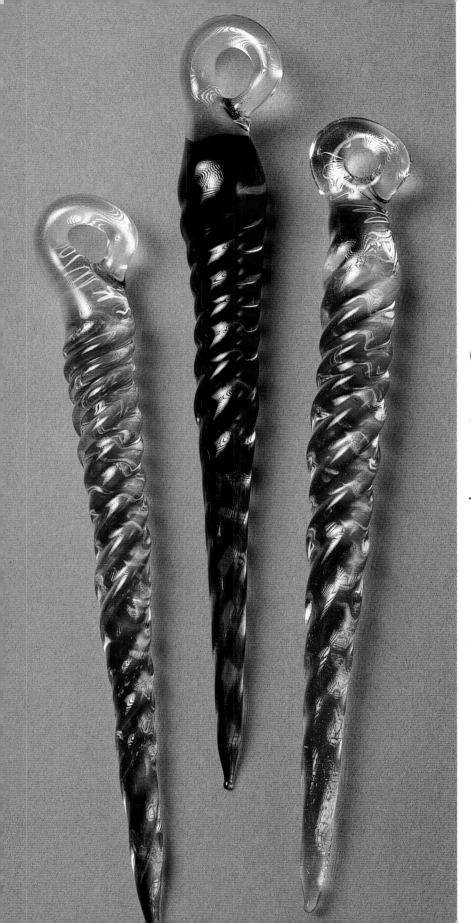

exercise 9—
MAKING ICICLES WITH COLORED STRIPES

This exercise allows you to work with color in a very creative way by fusing colored glass to clear glass. You'll learn to pull and twist the glass simultaneously to create a graduated form that is wide in diameter at one end and small at the other. Use one or several colors in each icicle. To familiarize yourself with all of the steps involved, consider practicing this exercise a few times with a clear glass rod before you add the color.

materials

Clear borosilicate rods:

6-10, 4 mm x 8 inches (20.3 cm) long

2, 7 mm x 12-15 inches (30.5-38.1 cm) long

2, 10 mm x 8 inches (20.3 cm) long

2, 12 mm x 12-15 inches (30.5-38.1 cm) long

Assortment of colored glass rods of your choice

tools

Tweezers

¼-inch (6 mm) graphite reamer

1. Clean up the end of a 12 mm rod. At the end of the flame, warm 3 inches (7.6 cm) opposite the turning end (photo 1).

2. As in exercise 5 on page 64, lay a stripe of color on the rod (photo 2).

3. Fuse three more stripes of color to the clear rod, spacing them evenly around the rod. Don't forget to press the color into the clear rod as it flows on. Fuse each stripe after you have applied it before you add the next one (photo 3).

4. Make sure that all of the colored stripes are fused well onto the clear rod (photo 4). (They don't need to be flattened into the clear rod to be fused.)

5. Attach a 10 mm rod to the end of the striped rod. Center it, align it with the 12 mm rod, and fuse it well. Keep rotating the rods as you do this (photo 5).

6. Begin heating the striped rod at the end where the color starts. To keep the rod centered and straight, align your hands as perfectly as possible while you rotate the glass. When the glass softens enough to begin moving, start rotating your D hand slightly faster than your ND hand, causing the glass to twist (photo 6). (You're now balancing the area of molten glass between two solid rods.)

7. Move down the striped rod, and continue to rotate and twist as you create a continuous spiral of color down the rod (photo 7). Don't twist the glass too quickly or tightly, since creases will form

4

5

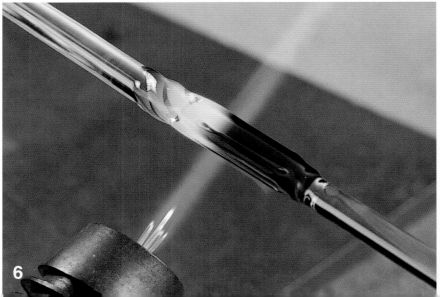

6

7

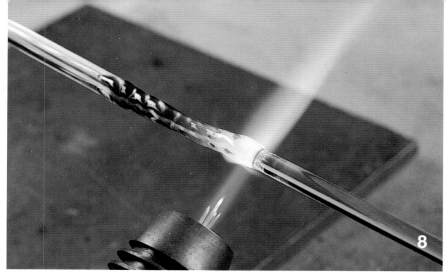

between the colored stripes. As you do this, begin to pull slightly with your D hand to stretch and thin the glass as you twist it (photo 8).

8. Continue this process until you've moved down the rod, twisting and thinning the rod to a point at the end (photo 9).

9. Remove the 10 mm rod and any excess glass from the tip end of the icicle (photo 10). Attach a punty to that end (photo 11).

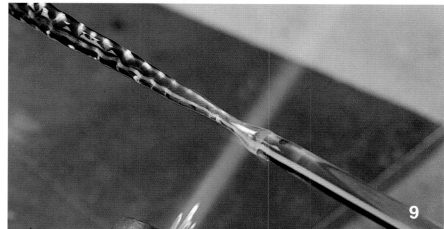

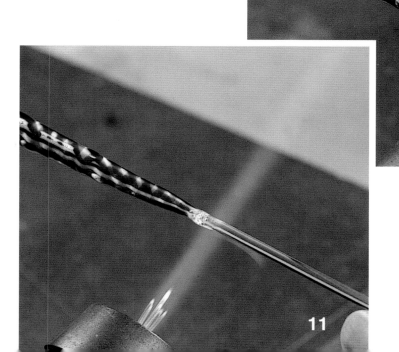

12

10. Now you're ready to remove the icicle from the 12 mm rod. Heat the rod at the top end of the stripes, and use the clear glass that you're removing to create a loop as you did in exercise 2 (photos 12 to 15).

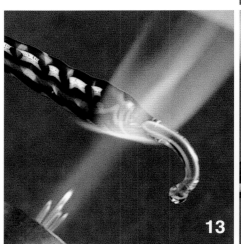

13

14

15

11. Hold the icicle in the air on the reamer, and allow it to cool (photo 16). After it cools, remove the punty in the flame (photo 17). Clean up the tip where you removed the punty.

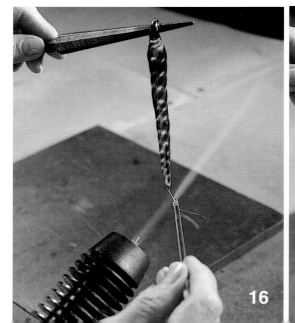

16

17

exercise 10—
WORKING WITH TUBING

Tubing comes in long pieces from the manufacturer. Before working with it, you'll need to cut the pieces into two halves so that you can handle it more easily. You can do this by cutting it with hot glass or by "pulling a point"–a common technique for manipulating tubing.

cutting tubing with hot glass

This first method of cutting tubing is the simplest. (This method doesn't work well for heavy-walled tubing.)

pulling a point

This technique creates "handles" and a "blowpipe" in a section of tubing in preparation for making something else from the glass. The handles allow you to hold a section of tubing while working with it, and the blowpipe allows you to control pressure inside the tube of softened glass so that it can be shaped and formed at the torch.

centering and straightening a point

You won't be able to pull perfect points in the beginning. If the point you make is straight but not centered (closer to one wall of the tubing than the other), you must center it before going further. If you don't, the next point you pull won't be centered either, and the object you make won't be symmetrical. If your point is centered but not straight, you must also correct this problem. You'll learn how to do this in the latter part of this exercise along with how to pull a second point.

materials

25 mm standard-wall tubing in clear borosilicate glass

1 clear borosilicate rod, 4 mm x 8 inches (20.3 cm) long

tools

Glass scoring knife

Black permanent marker

cutting tubing with hot glass

1. To begin, hold the tubing over your workbench, and balance it horizontally with one hand to find the balance point. Mark the spot with the black permanent marker, then scratch a ½- to 1-inch (1.3-2.5 cm) score line with your cutting tool at the marked spot (photos 1 and 2).

2. Adjust your torch to a medium-sized, hot flame.

3. Spit on your finger, and wipe it on the score line. (Doing this will help to heat shock the glass when you apply a hot rod to it in step 5 to follow.)

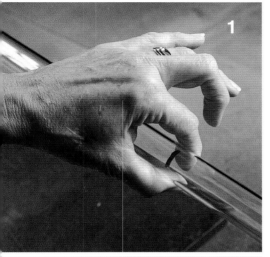

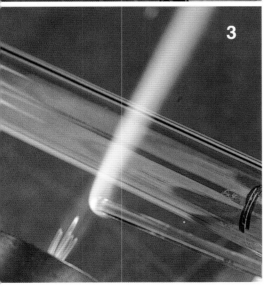

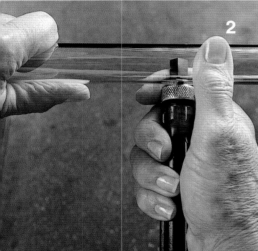

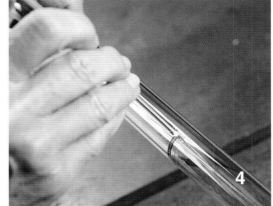

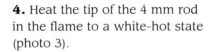

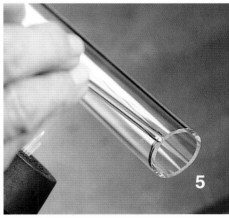

4. Heat the tip of the 4 mm rod in the flame to a white-hot state (photo 3).

5. Immediately place the hot end of the rod at one end of the score line, and press hard. You should see a crack begin to form and run around the tubing (photo 4). Half of the tubing will drop to your workbench, leaving you two shorter sections with which to work (photo 5).

pulling a point

1. Find the horizontal balance point on the tubing, and mark it with the black permanent marker.

2. Grip half of the tubing halfway between the balance spot and one end of it with your ND hand and an overhand grip, and hold the other half in the same way with your D hand and an underhand grip.

3. Set your torch to a wide, bushy flame with soft edges—not too hot. (You need a soft flame, since it helps to prevent hot spots on the tubing while you

heat it.) The flame should be about 1 inch (2.5 cm) wide, if possible.

4. At its balance point, begin rotating the tubing horizontally at the end of the flame, and gradually bring it down into the flame (photos 6 and 7).

5. Continue to turn the tubing horizontally in the flame. As it becomes soft, you may have a moment of panic because you

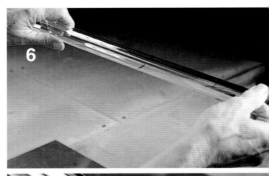

may feel as though you've lost control (photo 8). Neverthess, balance each half, and keep them lined up as you continue to turn. (Try not to twist the tubing.) Also, as the tubing gets soft and begins to move, you may want to respond by pulling the tubing apart. DO NOT DO THIS. Instead, think "push together, push together, push together," because your goal is to thicken up the walls of the tubing and collapse them slightly before you begin to pull. Keep turning.

6. Once you see that the tubing wall has thickened and the diameter of the tube has collapsed somewhat, lift the tubing out of the flame, and turn the tubing one or two full times. (This allows a skin to form on the surface of the glass.) Keep the tubing horizontal, begin to pull gently and slowly as you're turning to form the "shoulder" of the point—the area where the glass begins to change from a tube into a point (photo 9). Pull gradually to keep the point centered on the tube.

7. Once the shoulder is formed, begin pulling harder and faster while you keep turning (photo 10). Until this point, you've kept the glass horizontal. However, if you are trying to pull a long

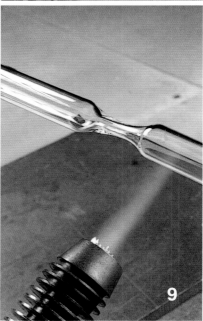

point, and you have short arms, you may find it difficult to pull in this position. After the shoulder of the point is formed, you can hold the tubing vertically, if needed. You may also want to do this part standing up rather than sitting.

8. As the glass begins to set up, pull very hard to keep the point straight. (If you don't keep strong tension in the glass, the point will curve.)

9. After the glass has totally set up, fire-cut the point in the flame, halfway between the two sections of tubing (photo 11). Points should be between 8 to 10 inches (20.3-25.4 cm) long or longer.

centering and straightening a point

1. Set your torch to a small, soft-edged flame about ¼ inch (6 mm) wide. Hold the tubing in your ND hand with an overhand grip. Turn the tubing, and use the flame to heat the shoulder of the point where it curves away from the straight tubing (photo 12).

2. Keep turning. Watch the shoulder as you turn it. It will appear to move up and down repeatedly.

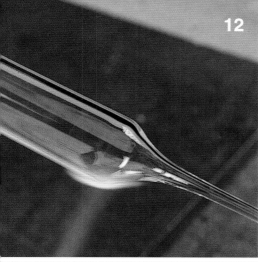

12

13

5. To begin straightening, turn and heat the glass where the slope of the shoulder ends and the point begins (photo 13).

6. Heat the glass until it softens and thickens. Rotate it in the flame while you lightly balance the point in your D hand. Atmospheric pressure will tend to center the point and straighten it up for you. Move the glass in and out of the flame to maintain control as you continue to turn the glass.

pulling a second point

1. To pull a second point, skip about 3 inches (7.6 cm) of tubing between the first and the section where you'll pull a second one. Pull the point, and cut it with the flame (photos 14, 15, and16).

2. To prepare the tubing for use, you need to open up the end of the tubing again, since both points were fused together in the flame. This creates an open system that allows the air to flow back and forth in the tube as it is heated and cooled. (If you put the ends in the flame without opening them, the molten glass will get sucked into the tube due to the vacuum that formed as the air cooled inside.) To open one end of the tubing, score the tip of one of the points with your knife, and break it off (photo 17). Now you have an open system that allows the air to move freely through the cut tip (photo 18).

3. When the shoulder has softened in the flame and is in an "up" position, remove it from the flame. Immediately move the point straight down at an angle that is 90° in reference to the straight side of the tubing. Don't bend the shoulder at an angle, but move it enough so that the point is on the center of the tubing.

4. To straighten a point, use the same flame that you used to center a point. As you undertake this process, you'll constantly turn the glass, whether you have it in the flame or out of the flame.

14

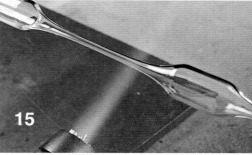

15

16

17

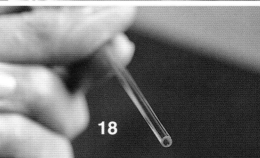

18

exercise 11—
MAKING A
CANDLEHOLDER

*I*n this exercise, you'll make a candleholder that can be assembled with a variety of candlesticks. You'll learn one of the methods for removing points to open up tubing so that you can make something from it.

Here, you won't heat the tubing in order to blow it into another shape, but you'll use the straight shape of the tube as it is. Because you don't have to control the shape as you blow, this makes a good exercise for beginning flameworkers.

materials

25 mm standard-wall tubing in clear borosilicate glass

tools

Glass scoring knife

Permanent black marker

Glass-cutting scissors

Large graphite reamer

Finger tool/claw holder

Graphite paddle

Tweezers

instructions

1. Pull two points with a section of tubing between them that is about 2 inches (5.1 cm) long (photo 1). (You can actually make your candleholder any height you wish, but one made from this length of tubing is nice.)

2. Make certain that both points are as centered as possible. If they aren't, take a bit of time to center them.

3. Choose the most centered point, and open the tip of it with your glass scoring knife. (This end will become the bottom of your candleholder.)

4. Hold the open end in your ND hand, and begin to heat the other point where it joins the shoulder, turning it as you go (photo 2). (Make sure to turn the glass anytime

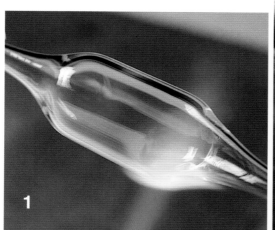

1

2

you put it into the flame.) When the glass is soft enough, pull the point off (photo 3). The glass should now be closed where the point was.

5. Place the closed end in the flame, and keep turning it (photo 4). When it becomes glowing red/white, remove it from the flame, and keep turning it.

6. Immediately bring the opened point to your mouth, and blow hard as you keep turning. Blow a very large bubble out the heated, closed end of the tubing (photo 5). The bubble will be large, very thin, and uneven.

7. Lower the piece with bubble intact into your dropoff bucket, then tap the bubble against the side of the can to break it off (photo 6). You now have a section of opened tubing that will become your candleholder, although it needs cleaning up.

8. To clean up the opened end, hold it in your ND hand, place the edge of it into the flame, and continue turning (photo 7). If the edge is very uneven, you may need to heat and soften the glass

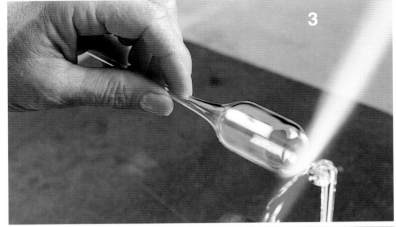

before using your scissors to trim off some of the excess (photo 8). You can also heat the opened end and press it against your graphite paddle to help smooth and even it (photo 9).

9. Now you can flare out the opened end a bit. Hold the tubing in your ND hand, and rotate it while placing the opened edge into a soft, hot flame. Heat the edge until it is soft.

10. Aim the flame at the bottom of the opening, and place the graphite end of your flaring tool just beneath the top edge (photo 10). Spin the candleholder evenly and quickly while resting the holder on the flaring tool. Don't push with the flaring tool—you're using it to hold the candleholder while the other hand is spinning.

11. Once again, press the opened edge against the graphite paddle.

12. If the opened end is still very uneven after shaping, use your tweezers and create a decorative edge as you did in the leaf exercise (on page 53). When treating the edge of a candleholder, work from one side to the opposite side and back again, rather than starting at one point and going all the way around. This will help you to evenly space the decorative edges around the opening of the candleholder.

13. Open your finger tool/claw holder, and put it in the opened end of the candleholder. Tighten it down, so that it grips the piece.

14. Set the torch to a narrow, soft flame. Hold the claw holder in your ND hand, and rotate the glass in the flame (photo 11). Cut off the remaining point far enough down—at least 1 inch (2.5 cm)—so that you can gather a ball of glass back up to the bottom of the candleholder that is large enough and strong enough for attaching it to something else (photos 12 and 13).

15. Set aside the candleholder for attaching to a candlestick later on (see the project on page 115). You can anneal the candleholder at this stage if you like.

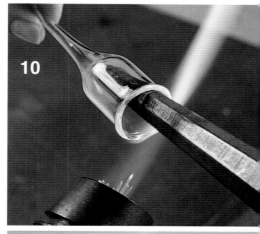

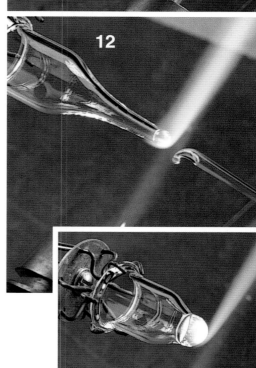

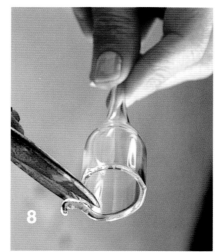

the projects

In the following projects, you'll use the skills that you've developed from doing the exercises. The objects that you made—such as leaves, fish, and flowers—will be assembled into larger, more sculptural pieces.

Since you'll be combining objects into final pieces, everything that you make has to be annealed when you finish making it. It's best to anneal your pieces as quickly as possible.

An annealing kiln is extremely hot, so wear protective clothing made of cotton or wool. Wear only closed-toe shoes in your studio and while you're working at the flame. You can also purchase special sleeves to slip on that protect your clothing and arms.

When placing things in the kiln, wear your heat-protective gloves, and, if needed, use a pair of large tweezers. You have to be even MORE careful when you take things out of the kiln, since the pieces will be very hot.

Different flameworkers run their annealing cycles in different ways, according to their personal preferences. There are some who keep their kilns at a lower temperature until they fill the kiln, and then they run the temperature up to the desired temperature.

I keep my holding kiln at 1050°F (566°C), so that I can take pieces in and out as I work on them. Since I have a kiln with a slotted door, the rod stays cool while the work gets annealed each time the piece goes in. If you have made your pieces well, they can go right into a kiln at the annealing temperature without cracking.

Here's a rule of thumb to follow for how long to leave the items inside the kiln: For small items such as a leaf, five minutes at annealing temperature is probably enough. For larger items, you should anneal for at least 30 minutes. Thankfully, you can't overdo annealing! In the case of borosilicate glass, you can take it out of the kiln once the glass has cooled down below 900°F (484°C).

As a beginner, you'll have to experiment with your kiln settings to decide which works best for you based on the way you work and the pieces you make. Remember, no amount of annealing will prevent cracks from forming in poorly made glass, or heal cracks if they are in the glass.

project 1—
VERSATILE PLANT STAKES

This project will teach you more about fusing two pieces of glass together effectively. If you don't fuse the parts together well, nothing you make will hold together.

You'll use leaves and other small objects that you made in the exercises to attach to the end of rods that can be used as plant stakes, drink stirrers, or a simple bouquet of shapes.

Choose shapes without loops on them to attach to the 7 mm rods. The rods can vary in length, although 8 to 10 inches (20.3-25.4 cm) long works well. You can attach a shape by its base or side, whichever you find more aesthetically pleasing.

materials

Several clear borosilicate rods, 7 mm x 8-10 inches (20.3-25.4 cm) long

Leaves, flowers, and other shapes with punties attached (see exercises 2, 3, 6, 7, and 8 for possibilities)

tools

¼-inch (6 mm) graphite rod (optional)

Wooden block with holes

instructions

1. Clean and fire-polish one end of a 7 mm rod. Hold the rod in your ND hand with an overhand grip.

2. With your D hand in an underhand grip, hold one of the shapes by the punty attached to the tip. Gently warm the shape by holding it slightly above a gentle, bushy flame (keeping in mind that heat rises). Rotate it, and warm it for a minute or two. (By doing this, you'll prevent heat shock when the shape is attached to the rod.)

3. If you plan to attach the shape by its base, gradually move the shape down toward the torch with the base of it just inside the flame's edge.

4. Hold the polished end of the rod in the other side of the flame. Rotate both the rod and shape back and forth as you heat them on opposite sides of the flame (photo 1).

5. When both pieces have reached a white-hot state, take them out of the flame, and stick them together quickly. (If the glass is hot enough, you'll see the two glasses flow together as soon as they touch.) Hold them perfectly still and count to three, then pull slightly (photo 2). You'll stretch the glass a bit when you pull, and help prevent creases from forming.

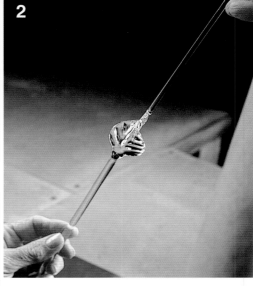

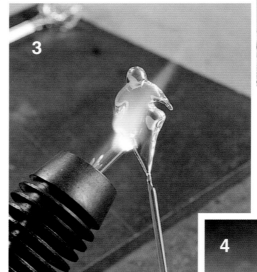

6. If you want to attach a shape by its side, don't rotate the shape as you heat it. Hold the edge in the flame, and heat it where you want to attach it to the rod (photos 3 and 4).

7. If you end up with creases where the two pieces join (this happens especially if the pieces weren't hot enough when you put them together), heat the glass where the crease is until it flows together and is gone. (If you have trouble seeing a crease,

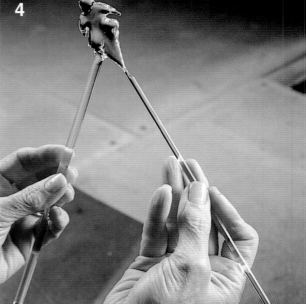

rub a knife blade on the surface of the glass to feel sharp indentations.) Take the piece out of the flame, and hold it perfectly still until the glass has set up.

8. Remove the punty from the tip.

9. As you did in step 2, gently warm the shape and section where it's attached to the rod for a couple of minutes.

10. Put the rod in your wooden block, and allow the shape to cool. (If you plan to add shapes to several rods, go ahead and do it now so that you can allow them to cool all at once.)

11. Once the shapes have cooled, fire-polish the ends of the rods to finish them (photo 5).

12. To lend a decorative touch, add a small ball on the end of the rod, flatten it with your ¼-inch (3 mm) graphite rod, and bend it at an angle to make a spoonlike end (photos 6 and 7).

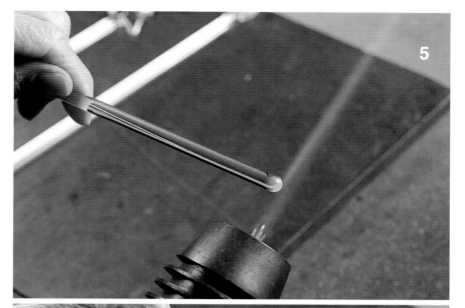

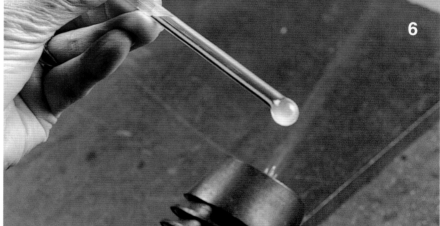

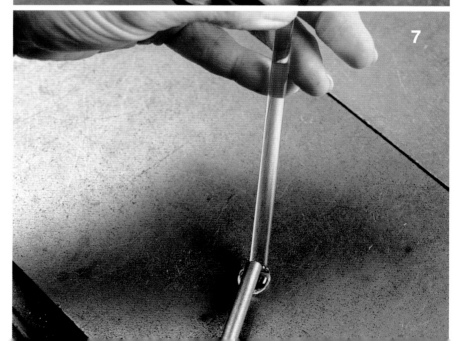

project 2—
FLOWERS WITH LEAVES AND STEMS

In this project, you'll attach a daisy-like flower to a stem, and add one or two leaves. Again, you'll use the technique of adding bridges (see exercise 8) to hold the sculpture together while you carefully fuse all the joints.

materials for one flower

Glass flower and 2 leaves with punties attached (see exercises 3 and 8 on pages 53 and 78 for instructions)

Clear borosilicate glass rods:

2, 4 mm x 15 inches (38.1 cm) long

1, 7 mm x 12-15 inches (30.5-38.1 cm) long

tools

Tweezers

instructions

1. Clean up the end of one of your 7 mm rods. Hold the premade flower by the punty that is attached to the tip of a petal, and fuse the base of it to the end of the 7 mm rod or stem (photo 1). Remove the punty.

2. Fuse one of the 4 mm rods to the tip of one of your petals (photo 2). Bend it down so that it touches the bottom of the stem, and fuse it in place to form a bridge. Skip the petal next to the first one, and attach another bridge (photo 3).

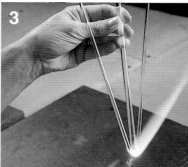
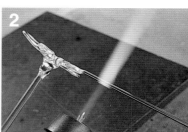

3. Thoroughly fuse the end of the piece where the bridges meet the center (photo 4).

4. Thoroughly fuse the flower to the top of the stem (photo 5). Move around the joint with the flame, making sure that there are no creases and that the two pieces of glass become one.

5. Next you'll attach a leaf to the stem close to the top. Heat the end of it in the flame in preparation for fusing it to the stem (photo 6). Rather than removing the punties attached to the tips of the leaves, connect them to the other bridges that hold the flower to the bottom of the stem (photo 7). This system will hold them in place while you fuse them well to the stem (photo 8).

6. Now that you've assembled the flower, check all of the joints and make sure that you don't see any creases or devitrification. If you see either, take care of these problems before you go any further (see pages 23 to 26 for more information).

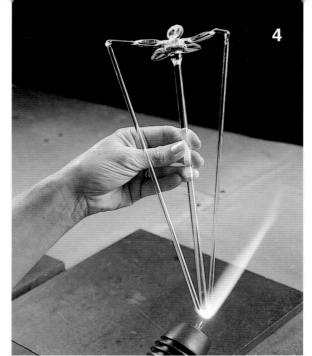

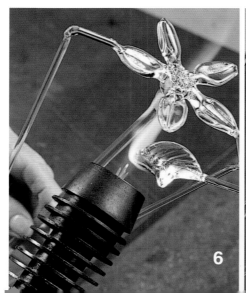

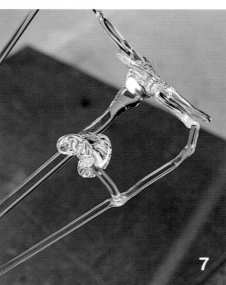

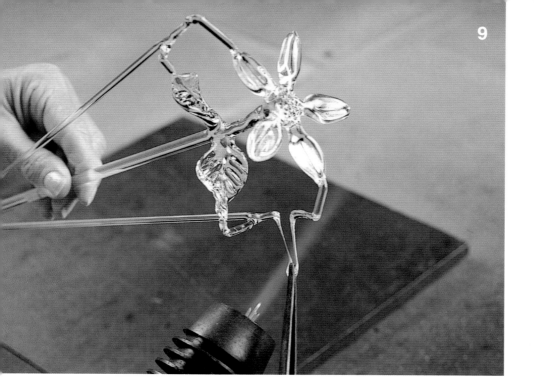

9

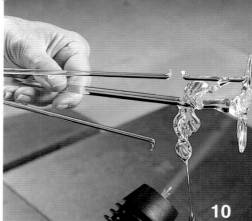

10

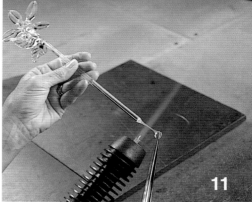

11

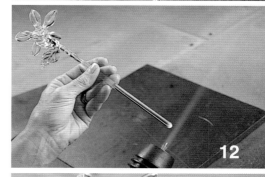

12

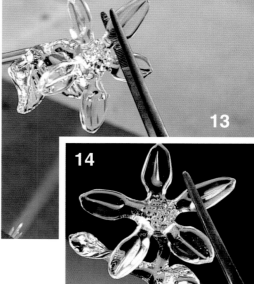

13

14

7. Wait for the glass to cool so that you can remove the bridges. (Since the bridges are attached to the tips of the leaves and petals, you'll heat a very small amount of glass to prevent cracking when you remove them.) Heat a spot in the center of each bridge, and remove the molten glass with your tweezers, leaving a gap (photo 9).

8. Heat the tip of each petal, and pull away the excess glass that formed each bridge. Do the same for each leaf (photo 10).

9. If you need to reshape some tips of petals and leaves, heat each to molten, take it out of the flame, and touch it with a cold 4 mm rod before pulling out the excess glass. Fire-cut the thread near the tip, and fuse the remaining glass back into it.

10. Fire-polish the other end of the 7 mm rod (photos 11 and 12).

11. Repeat the steps outlined to make as many flowers as you wish. Suggestions for variations: Make flower heads with different sizes of glass to create various sizes to be put together in your bouquet. If you wish, heat and bend some of the petals so that they aren't perfectly straight (photos 13 and 14). Try adding petals in two rows, alternating the lower row with those in the first row. Try bending and shaping the petals before attaching them and, in another flower, after you add them.

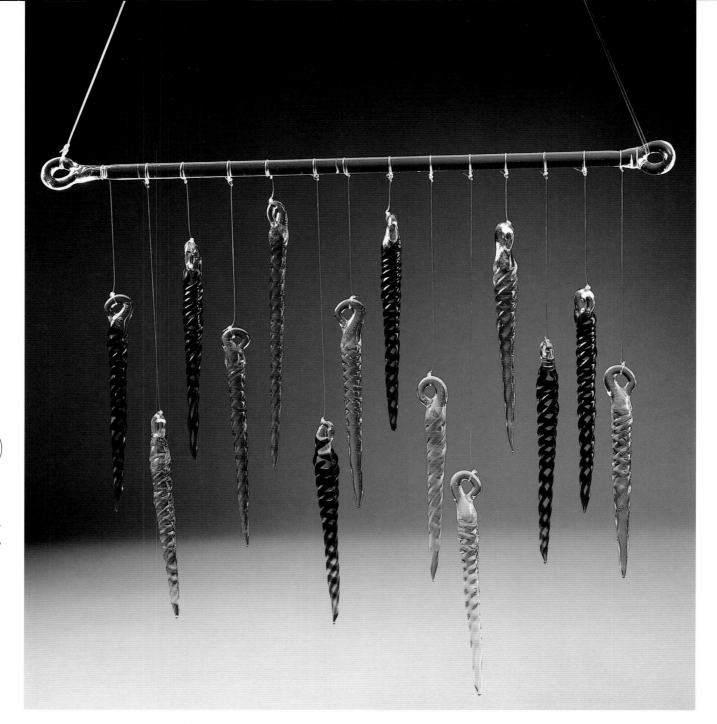

project 3—
COLORFUL SUNCATCHER

In this project, you'll attach a set of the colored icicles to a glass rod with loops added. The assemblage can then be hung against a window to reflect light.

materials

Several colored, striped icicles (see exercise 9 on page 84)

Clear borosilicate glass rods:

7 mm x 10 inches (25.4 cm)

10 mm x 12 inches (30.5 cm) long

25-gauge monofilament or lightweight string

tools

Regular scissors

Tweezers

Tungsten pick

Graphite rod or small graphite reamer

Ruler

instructions

1. Clean up and fire-polish both ends of the 10 mm rod, and set it aside to cool.

2. Adjust your torch to a small, soft flame. With your ND hand, hold the end of the 7 mm rod just above the flame to heat it. Don't rotate it.

3. The 7 mm rod will begin to soften and curl down. Allow gravity to do its work on the glass. As the rod softens and curls, move the flame farther down the rod toward the cut end, and allow that portion to curl down as well. (As you work on the rod, you might have to occasionally brush the top of it through the flame to heat it thoroughly.)

4. When the curled portion of the 7 mm rod resembles a hook, take your tweezers in your D hand, grab the end of it, and bring it around so that it touches the straight portion of the rod (photo 1). Heat the end of the rod, and press it with the help of a tungsten pick or tweezers (photo 2).

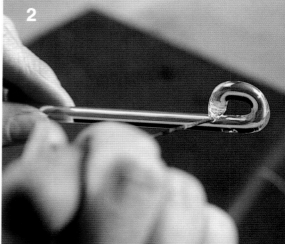

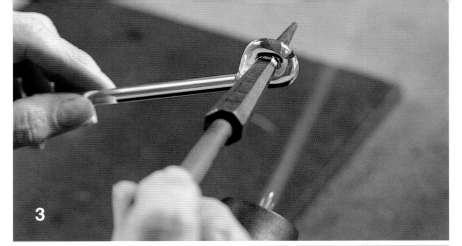

5. With a small flame, fuse the end of the 7 mm curled rod to the straight portion of the rod.

6. Increase the flame a bit. Hold the 7 mm rod with the loop on it in your ND hand. Hold the ¼-inch (6 mm) graphite rod or the small graphite reamer in your D hand. Aim the flame directly through the hole formed by the curved portion of the rod so the glass begins to shrink down.

7. Remove the loop from the flame, and before the loop hole closes, insert the pointed end of the graphite rod or small graphite reamer into it. Rotate it in order to round out the hole (photos 3 and 4). You may need to do this several times.

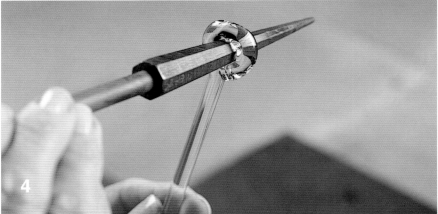

8. Attach a punty to the top of the loop, and remove the loop from its turning rod. Heat the area where the curved portion of the loop joins the straight portion of the rod to make sure the fuse is complete. Use the graphite rod or small graphite reamer to round out the loop hole for a final time, leaving the punty attached. Use the same procedure to make another identical loop with the remaining 7 mm rod.

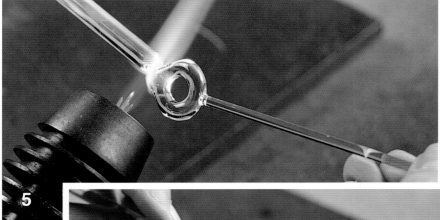

9. Attach one of the loops to the end of the 10 mm rod, and fuse it well (photos 5 and 6). On the opposite end of the rod, attach the other loop so that it lines up

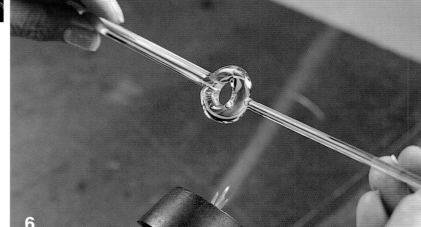

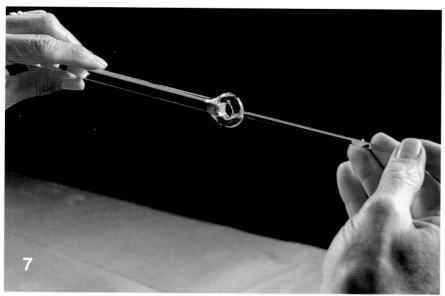

7

with the first one (photo 7). Remove the punties. Place the rod with loops attached into your annealing kiln.

10. Thread a piece of monofilament or string through each of the loops on the rod, and tie the ends so that you can hang the rod. Hang and stabilize it in preparation for positioning the icicles.

11. Cut and tie a length of monofilament or string, each around 8 to 10 inches (20.3-25.4 cm) in length (photo 8), to each icicle that you plan to hang. On either end of the rod, tie on an icicle so that it's counterbalanced (photo 9). (It needn't be level at this point.)

12. Tie on the remaining icicles in a pleasing arrangement that ends up horizontally balanced, adjusting the strings as needed (photo 10).

8

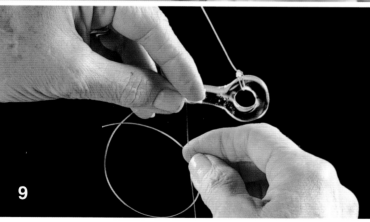

9

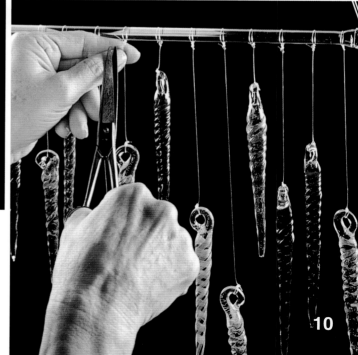

KINETIC LEAF MOBILE

In this project, you'll use leaves with loops attached to create a mobile that is delightful when a breeze catches its shining leaves. You can use colored or clear leaves or a combination of both.

materials

18-20 glass leaves with attached loops (see exercises 2 and 3 on pages 45 and 53)*

*If you don't want to use clear leaves, you can decorate the leaves by laying on a color stripe in the center, and/or putting color around the edge of the flattened disc before you pull it into the leaf shape. You can also add colored dots or frit to the surface. (Anytime you add color, make sure to fuse it really well.) Add decorative edges as described in the exercise.

tools

6-inch (15.2 cm) wood or metal embroidery hoop

Black permanent marker

Red permanent marker

Measuring tape or ruler

Regular scissors

25-gauge monofilament or lightweight string

instructions

1. Use the measuring tape and the black marker to mark your wood or metal hoop at 1-inch (2.5 cm) intervals all the way around. Use the red marker to make three marks on the hoop that form a triangular shape if you're looking down at the hoop. Space these marks between the ones you've made with the black marker (photo 1).

2. Tie a 12-inch (30.5 cm) piece of monofilament or string to the three colored marks. Holding the hoop aloft, bring the ends together with one hand, balance the hoop so that it's horizontal, and tie a knot at the top about 6 to 8 inches (15.2-20.3 cm) above the hoop. Adjust the knot as needed so that the hoop hangs straight (photo 2).

3. Tie a 10-inch (25.4 cm) length of monofilament or string to one of your leaves. Secure the knot by tying it several times, then clip the short end about ¼ inch (6 mm) from the knot. Tie the other end to the hoop at one of the marks (photo 3) so that the length of monofilament from the hoop to the leaf is approximately 4 inches (10.2 cm).

4. Repeat this process with each of your leaves, adding 1 inch (2.5 cm) to the monofilament or string between the hoop and the leaf (photo 4). You'll end up with a spiral of leaves circling down from the hoop (photo 5).

5. After you've attached leaves to all the marks on the hoop, tie a piece of monofilament to the knot at the top for hanging.

Note: You can use the above idea with any glass shapes that you've made, or combine glass with natural materials, such as shells.

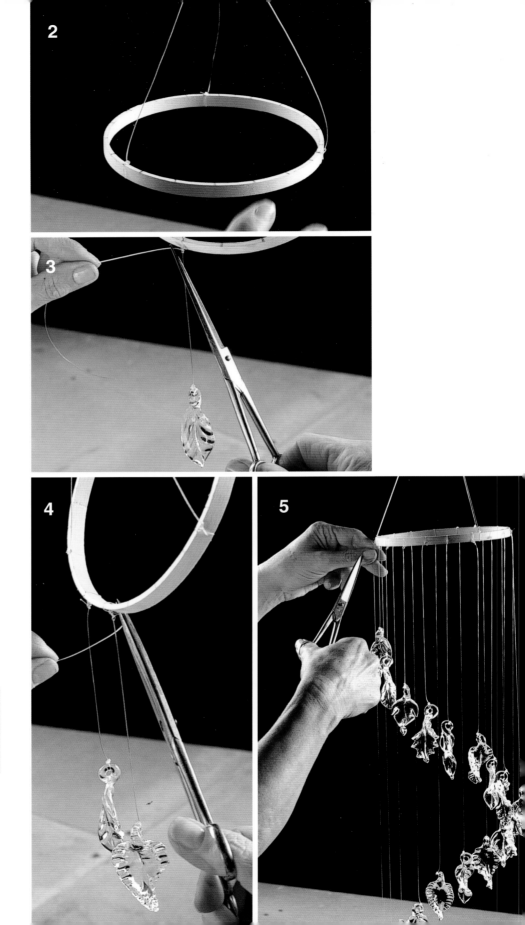

project 5—
CANDLESTICK WITH
TRANSITIONAL SHAPES

In this project you'll make a simple candlestick. By making this piece, you'll learn about the sequence of activities needed to assemble a larger sculptural shape. The design of the rod can be varied if you don't want to make one that looks exactly like ours.

When making an object such as this candlestick, you must be aware of the center of gravity. If it is too high, the piece can tip over, especially when you add more height with a candle. It's good to create a low center of gravity by making the piece short (fewer transitional shapes), the base very wide (bigger or longer leaves), or add more weight to the bottom (add a large ball or thick, heavy leaves). For a truly stable candlestick, do all three. Evaluating the center of gravity requires finding a balance between design and aesthetics.

materials

Clear borosilicate glass rods:

Several rods, 4 mm x 6-8 inches (15.2-20.3 cm) long

5 or 6 rods, 12 mm x 12-15 inches (30.5-38.1 cm) long

12 mm colored borosilicate rods in red and blue

Length of 25 mm tubing

tools

Dinner or paring knife

Tweezers

Wooden block with holes

Finger tool/claw holder

instructions

1. Make three clear leaves of approximately the same size and shape from a 12 mm rod, and use a knife to press veins into them (see exercise 3 on page 53). Leave the punty attached to each leaf. Stand the leaves up in your wooden block to cool.

2. Use a clear 12 mm rod to create a transitional series composed of a ball, three marias, and a ball (see exercise 4 on page 61). Remove the rod at one end.

3. Case 3 inches (7.6 cm) of two clear 12 mm rods with red and blue (see exercise 5 on page 64), and pull the rods to approximately 12 mm in preparation for making two balls from each color. To make four separate balls from the cased rods, create a ball at the end of the rod, attach a punty, remove the ball from the rod, and round up that side of the ball. Leave the punty attached to each ball, and stand them in your wooden block to cool.

4. Use the 25 mm glass tubing to make a candleholder in a size of your choice with a plain or decorated edge (see exercise 11 on page 94).

5. To assemble the candleholder, begin by holding the rod with the balls and marias in your ND hand. On one side of the flame, heat the ball on the end of the rod while you heat one of the colored balls on the other side of the flame (photo 1). (Heat only the area of each ball that will be joined with the other.) When both sides are hot, stick them together so that the colored ball is centered on the rod. (To avoid creases, count to three once they're stuck together, and then pull them apart slightly.) Remove the punty after fusing.

6. Add two more colored balls in a line, and remove the punty after fusing. Make sure that all the joints are fused together well (photos 2 and 3).

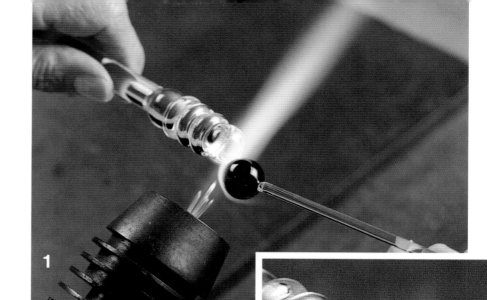

7. Pick up the candleholder with your finger tool/claw holder (photo 4). On one side of the flame, heat the remaining colored ball. Heat the ball at the bottom of the candleholder on the other side of the flame. When they're both hot, stick them together (photo 5). (As you do this, keep the glass rotating continuously in one direction, or back and forth if the glass becomes soft and begins to sag.

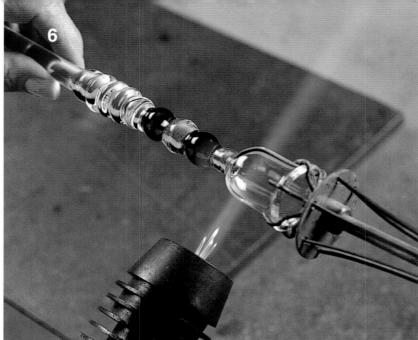

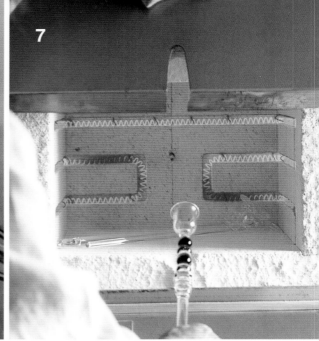

Make sure to keep it from going off-center.) Check to make sure that the candleholder is centered, straight, and well-fused to the candlestick so that a candle placed in it won't lean (photo 6).

8. Place the assembly in the kiln to anneal (photo 7). (If you have a holding kiln, you can leave the bottom 12 mm rod sticking out the door.)

9. After it has annealed, remove it from the holding kiln and allow it to cool until you can pick it up and hold it comfortably. Remove the turning rod.

10. Make a large ball on the end of a clear 12 mm rod. Attach the last colored ball to the top of the large clear ball opposite the turning rod, so that the colored ball is centered on the rod (photo 8).

11. Hold the turning rod in your ND hand and the candlestick in your D hand. Heat the colored

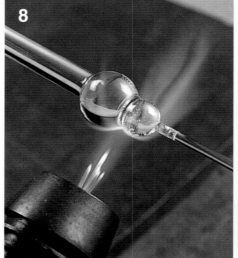

ball on one side of the flame and the clear ball at the end of the candlestick on the other side (photo 9). Keep rotating the pieces, moving them back and forth as needed. When they're hot, stick them together. Fuse the glass well to prevent creases (photo 10).

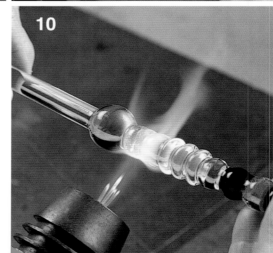

12. Remove the turning rod (photo 11). While the large ball is still hot, heat one leaf at a time at the end of the flame in prepation for fusing it to the ball. Space the leaves equally around the ball—halfway between the top and the bottom of the ball and attached at a 90° angle (photos 12 and 13). Remove the punties (photo 14)

13. Add a bridge system (if needed) to support the leaves while you fuse them into place on both the front and the back (photo 15).

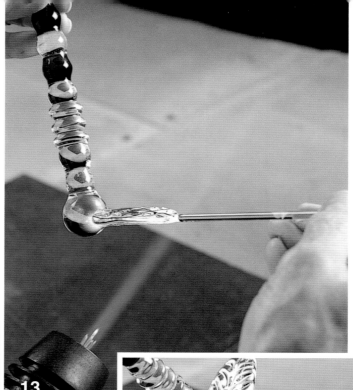

13

11

12

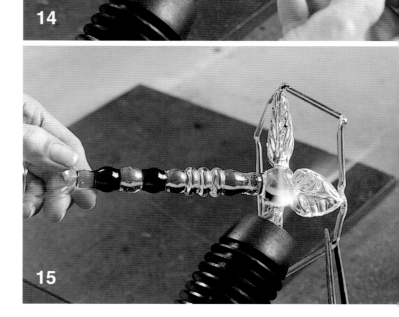

14

15

Remove the bridges after fusing (photos 16 and 17).

14. Heat each leaf close to where it is joined to the ball, but not at the point of fusion (photo 18). Bend each leaf slightly to create "feet" for the candlestick (photo 19).

15. Set the candlestick down on your workbench to check the stability of the feet. If a leaf needs to be changed, reheat it in the flame and soften it again before adjusting its position (photo 20). Hold it perfectly still while the glass sets up. Continue this process until the candlestick stands as straight as possible.

16. Quickly put the candlestick into the kiln to anneal. If the large ball at the bottom cools too rapidly, it will crack; therefore, you must work quickly. Experience will teach you the pace that you need to take.

16

17

18

19

20

project 6—
DECORATIVE
GLASS CANDIES

To make this project, you'll use beadmaking techniques to create three different candy designs. The underlying shape will remain the same, but you'll decorate the surfaces differently. The colors suggested below are a good variety of warm/cool and transparent/opaque.

Before you begin to make the candies, you'll pull "stringers" from each of the colored rods. Stringers are threadlike rods of glass used to create detailed decoration on the surface of other glass.

materials

Clear borosilicate rods:

Several rods, 7 mm x 8-10 inches (20.3-25.4 cm) long

Several rods, 10 mm x 12-15 inches (30.5 x 38.1 cm) long

Several rods, 12 mm x 12-15 inches (30.5 x 38.1 cm) long

Rods of borosilicate white glass as they come from manufacturer

Five assorted colored rods as they come from manufacturer

tools

Tweezers

instructions

1. Set your torch to a small, soft flame. Hold one of the colored rods in your ND hand with an overhand grip. Hold one of the 7 mm rods in your D hand with an underhand grip, and fuse the two together (photo 1).

2. Heat the end of the colored rod. As it becomes molten, begin to pull with your D hand, keeping the end of the colored rod in the flame. Continue to pull as a very thin rod of glass begins to string out (photo 2).

3. The size of the stringer that you create depends on how you control the heat and how quickly you pull. You may need to dip the end of the colored rod in and out of the flame to control the heat. (Try to get even heating and pulling so that the stringer will have a consistent size.) Continue to pull the stringer out as long as it is comfortable for you to do so. (You can probably pull a long enough stringer to get two 12-inch [30.5 cm] pieces from one pull.) Fire-cut the stringer (photo 3). Put it aside to cool.

4. Continue pulling stringers until you have two or three 12-inch (30.5 cm) ones from each of the colored rods.

5. When the stringers have cooled, remove the 7 mm rods if you haven't already done so.

6. Case a clear 12 mm rod with white glass (see exercise 5 on page 64), and fuse it well to the rod (photo 4). When you pull it out, allow the rod to be slightly thicker than 12 mm. Make several of these, and leave them attached to the 12 mm rods. Remove the rod at the other end.

7. Now you can decorate the rod with one of the three different methods described next.

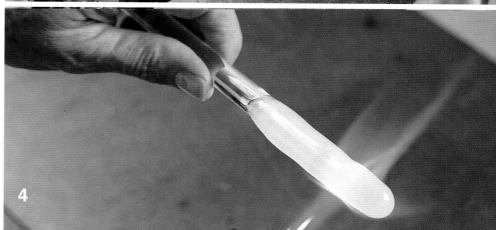

method #1

A. Choose two different colored stringers. Warm a 1-inch (2.5 cm) section of the white cased rod, and lay on alternating stripes of the colored stringers, leaving white between each color (photo 5). Hold the white rod just below a small, soft flame. Hold the end of the stringer in the flame, and press it to the glass as you move the white rod up. (This is the same method as laying on a stripe of color to case a rod, only the scale is different.)

B. Fuse the color to the surface of the white rod (photo 6). Attach a 10 mm clear rod, and begin to heat the cased rod at the 10 mm end (photo 7). As the glass softens, turn your D hand faster than your ND hand, causing the glass and the lines on the surface of it to twist (photo 8).

C. When you've heated and twisted the entire length of the stripes, remove it from the cased rod and follow steps 8 to 12 on page 126.

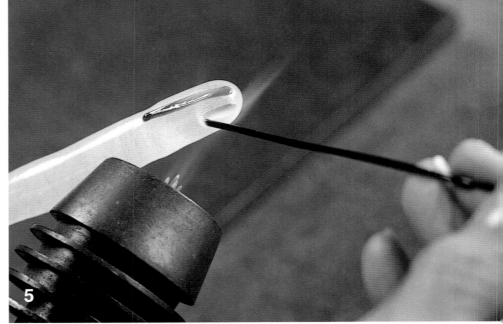

5

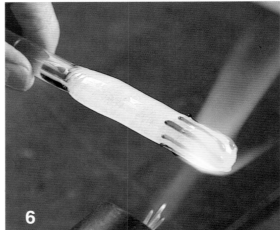

6

7

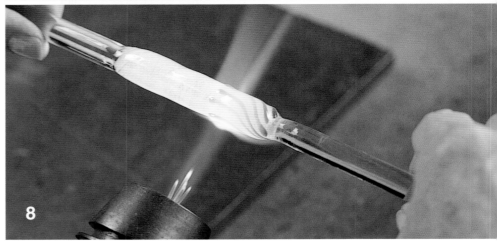

8

method #2

A. You might want to use all five colored stringers for this method. Begin by warming a 1-inch (2.5 cm) section of the cased rod as you did in method #1, then use one of the stringers to begin dotting on color at one end. As you move the color toward the other end, turn the rod slightly in your ND hand as you add each dot to create a spiral effect (photo 9).

B. Continue to add color with the stringers until you have completed the surface decoration (photo 10).

C. Fuse all of the dots thoroughly. Follow steps 8 to 12 on page 126.

method #3

A. For this method, you'll use three of the colored stringers. Warm a 1-inch (2.5 cm) section of the cased rod as you did in methods #1 and #2. With the first color, lay on three stripes that are evenly spaced around the warmed end of the cased rod.

B. With the second color, lay stripes to the right of and next to each of the ones you've already placed (photo 11).

C. Heat across the center of the two stripes simultaneously. Immediately remove the rod from the flame, and, with your tweezers, pinch the two stripes together and twist (photo 12). Do this with the remaining two sets of stripes.

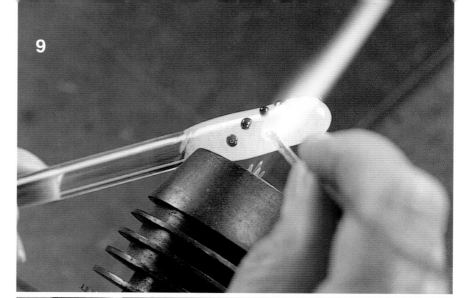

9

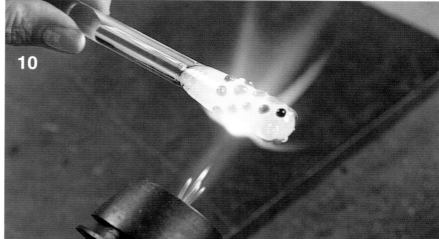

10

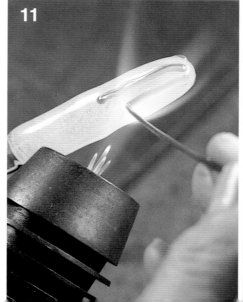

11

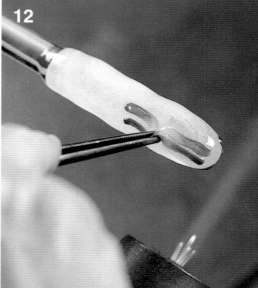

12

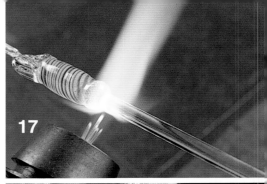

D. With the third color, lay a row of dots between each of the pairs of pinched stripes (photos 13 and 14). Finish the candy by following steps 8 to 12 below.

8. All of the glass candies are finished in the same fashion, as follows: First, remove the section of the cased white rod that is not decorated, leaving the "candy" portion of the piece.

9. Create a ball of glass on the end of a clear 7 mm rod, and fuse it to the end of the cased and decorated rod. Remove the 7 mm rod (photo 15).

10. Heat the clear glass that you've just added, and heat it well so that it's fused to the end of the rod and very hot. Take the rod out of the flame, hold it vertically, and pinch it with your tweezers about four times. Then grab the end and twist it (photo 16). Do this quickly before the glass has a chance to set up.

11. Attach a 4 mm punty to the twisted end. Hold the punty with your ND hand. To the other end of the candy, add another ball of clear glass (photo 17). Heat it as you did before, and when

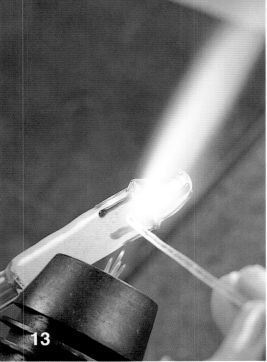

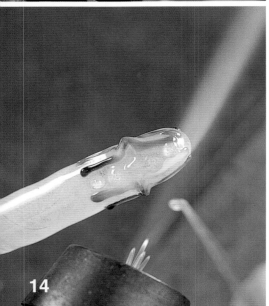

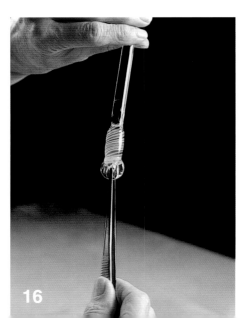

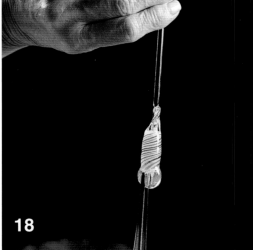

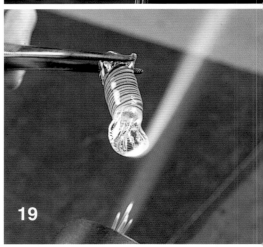

you pinch it with the tweezers, turn the glass so it is at a 90° angle to the other end (photo 18). Pinch the end with your tweezers, then grab and twist as you did before.

12. Remove the punty. Fire-polish the place where you removed the punty so that it blends into the candy (photo 19).

project 7—
BEADS AS
GLASS SCULPTURE

You can think of beads as beautiful small sculptures that are wearable. They can be simple or elaborate in their design and decoration. If you've never made them, you'll develop a new set of skills when you work with solid glass wrapped around a steel mandrel (rod).

The positioning of the mandrel and the glass rod is similar to that of rods when you case a clear one with color, but the movement is different. The mandrel is rotated just beneath the flame as you hold the rod in the flame to apply the glass.

In this project, you'll make three beads with different designs using some of the techniques learned in the previous project on making glass candies.

materials

1 clear borosilicate rod: 7 mm x 12 inches (30.5 cm) long

1 white glass rod: 7 mm x 12 inches (30.5 cm) long

4-6, 7 mm colored borosilicate rods in colors of your choice

7 mm colored rods in 4-6 colors of your choice that have been pulled into stringers that are about 12 inches (30.5 cm) long each

Jar of bead release (available through flameworking supplier)

tools

Several steel mandrels

Wooden block with holes

Holding kiln

Wide-bladed dinner knife

Graphite paddle

Tungsten pick

making the body of the bead

1. Dip the bottom 4 inches (10.2 cm) of several mandrels into the jar of bead release, and heat them at the end of the the flame to dry them (photos 1 and 2).

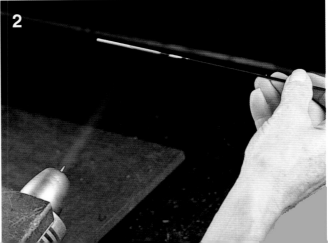

2. After the first coat of bead release has dried, allow the coated mandrel to cool, and then dip the mandrel into the bead release again to form a second layer. Dry the mandrel as you did in step 1.

3. Heat the end of the 7 mm clear rod at the edge of the flame (photo 3).

4. When the clear rod is in a white-hot state, touch it to the mandrel about 1½ inches (3.8 cm) from the end, and begin turning it immediately (photo 4). Continue to hold the mandrel under the flame. Keep the clear glass hot, and gradually wrap it around the mandrel with each new wrap slightly overlapping the edge of the previous one (photos 5 and 6).

5. Continue wrapping the glass around the mandrel until the length of glass is about 1 inch (2.5 cm). Remove the 7 mm clear glass rod.

6. Gently heat the glass(photo 7) and roll it on a graphite paddle until it is smooth (photo 8).

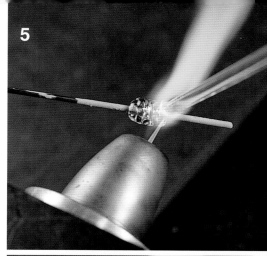

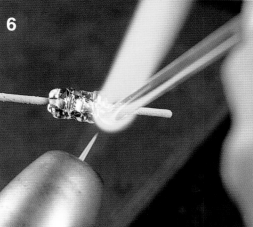

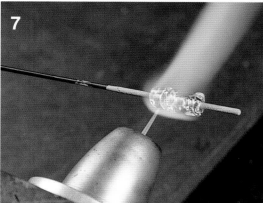

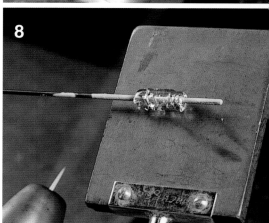

7. With a white rod approximatly 7 mm in diameter, repeat the above process, wrapping the white glass over the clear (photos 9 and 10).

8. Gently heat the glass to fuse the white to the clear. Roll it on the graphite paddle to smooth it out (photo 11).

9. Gently heat each end of the bead, and press it with a knife to even out any rough glass (photo 12). If you wish, add another layer of white to the piece.

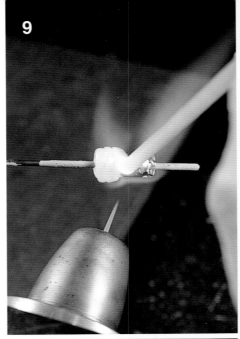

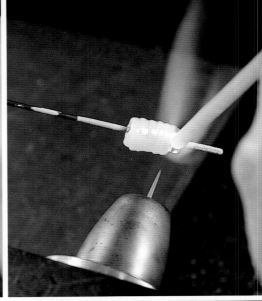

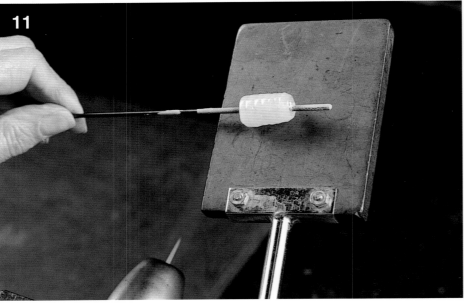

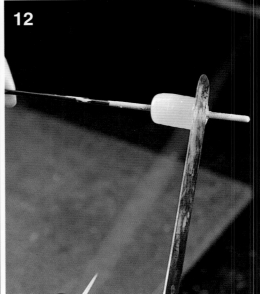

variation 1: bead with flowers

1. Select a colored rod for making flower petals. Keep the bead warm in the flame, and soften the end of the colored rod at the edge of the flame. Directly heat the spot where the petal will be applied, and then press the end of the rod into the bead. Add three more petals, and fuse them well on the surface of the bead (photos 13 and 14).

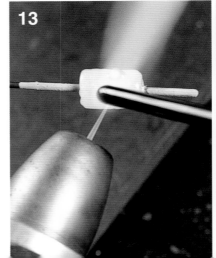

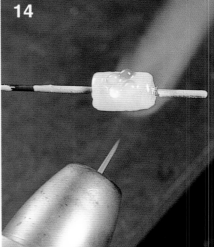

2. Use a contrasting stringer or rod to add a center to the flower (photo 15).

3. Select a colored rod for the leaves. At a place between two petals, heat the spot where you want to add a leaf. Press the soft tip of the colored rod into the surface of the glass to form a round dot of color (photo 16). Heat the dot before dragging the edge out with the tip of your tungsten pick to form the tip of a leaf (photo 17).

4. Turn the bead over, and repeat this process on the other side.

5. Place the finished bead on its mandrel in the annealing kiln. After annealing, remove it and allow it to cool. Gently slide the bead off the mandrel. (If it is difficult to remove, stand the mandrel up in a glass of ice water—the steel will contract and make the bead easier to remove.)

variation 2: layered dot bead

1. Make a bead body on a mandrel as you did at the beginning of this project.

2. Choose a 7 mm colored rod and a colored stringer that contrast and are aesthetically pleasing together.

3. Heat a spot in the middle of the bead, and use the rod to press on a dot of color. Repeat this step as you rotate the bead, spacing the dots evenly around the bead (photo 18). After you're finished, fuse them into place.

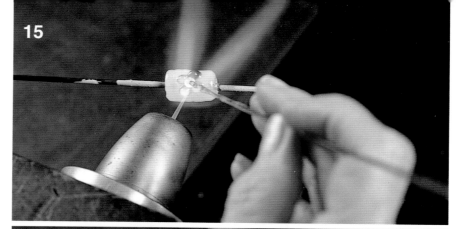

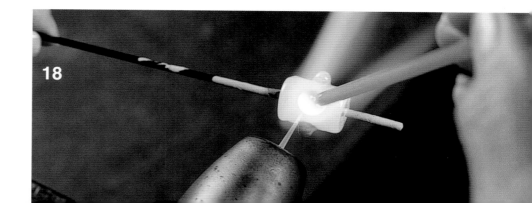

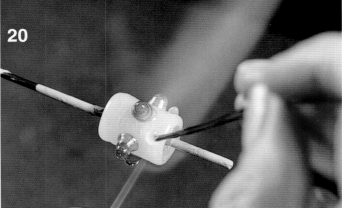

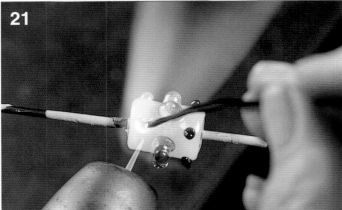

4. Use the contrasting stringer to place a dot of color on top of each of the larger dots (photo 19).

5. Heat the bead toward one end, and use a stringer of a third color to add an even row of

small dots around the end (photo 20). Repeat this step at the other end of the bead (photo 21).

6. After completing the bead, anneal it. Remove it from the mandrel as described in step 5 of variation 1.

variation 3: striped bead

1. Make a bead body on a mandrel as you did at the beginning of this project.

2. Choose two different colored stringers for decoration. Heat the bead, and lay on alternating stripes of color, leaving white glass between them (photos 22 and 23). Fuse the stripes well (photo 24).

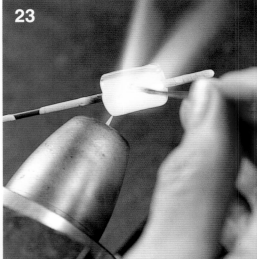

variation 3: continued

3. Hold the bead at the bottom of the flame, and heat across the stripes on the surface of the bead (photo 25).

4. When the glass is very soft, drag the tip of a tungsten pick through the surface of it, pulling the threads into a feathered design all the way around the bead (photo 26). Fuse the decoration well.

5. Roll it on the graphite paddle to smooth it out (photo 27).

6. Anneal the bead to finish it, then remove it from the mandrel.

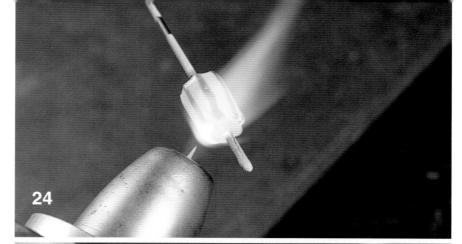

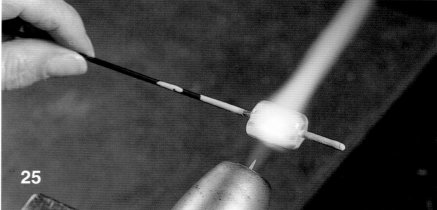

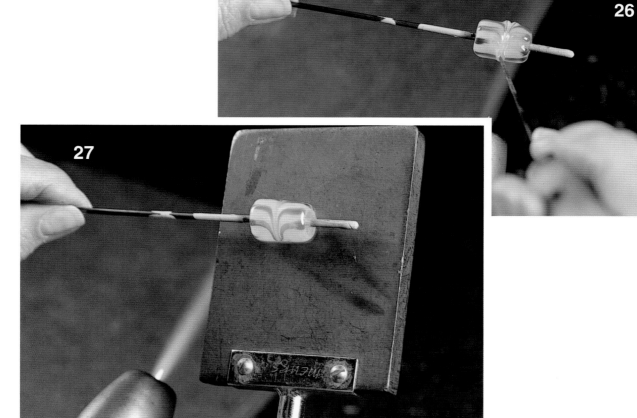

project 8—
TALL CANDLESTICK WITH FISH MOTIF

In this project, you'll combine several of the shapes you've already learned how to make into a tall, sculptural candlestick. You can use clear glass to make an elegant candlestick, or add color to the various parts.

materials

Clear borosilicate glass rods:

7, 4 mm x 6-8 inches (15.2-20.3 cm) long (for punties)

2, 4 mm x 12-15 inches (30.5-38.1 cm) long (for bridges)

2, 7 mm x 12-15 inches (30.5-38.1 cm) long

1,10 mm x 12-15 inches (30.5-38.1 cm) long

4,12 mm x 12-15 inches (30.5-38.1 cm) long

tools

Holding kiln

Finger tool/claw holder

Wooden block with holes

Graphite plate

instructions

1. With clear 12 mm rod, make three simple leaves of about the same size and shape (see exercise 2 on page 45). Leave the punties attached, and set the leaves aside in your wooden block.

2. From a 12 mm rod, make a fish body and attach a punty to the tail fin. Use the 7 mm clear rod to wipe on the fins and tail (see exercise 7 on page 72).

3. With a 7 mm rod, add a small ball of glass in front of or behind the back (dorsal) fin, and add a small ball of glass in the opposite position on the abdominal fin. Place these balls in line with one another, imagining these points attached to the candlestick later.

4. With the punty attached to the fish, place it into the holding kiln set at the annealing temperature of 1050°F (566°C) with the punty sticking out of the hole in the door. If you don't have an annealing kiln, do one of the following: Remove the punty, put the piece in a regular kiln. When you're ready to work with the fish again, use tweezers to retrieve it, and put the punty back on. If you don't use this method, warm the piece thoroughly for several minutes at the end of the flame before plunging it directly into the flame.

5. With a 10 mm clear rod, make five ball shapes in a row. (When you assemble the candlestick, you don't have to use the entire length if you don't want to.)

6. With a clear 12 mm rod, make a 4- to 5-inch (10.2-12.7 cm) section of marias and transitional shapes (see exercise 4 on page 61).

7. Make a large ball with a clear 12 mm rod. Attach the section of marias and transitional shapes to the large ball opposite the 12 mm turning rod to form the shaft of the candlestick (photo 1). Center the section you've added, and fuse it well (photo 2).

8. Remove the fish from the holding kiln, and hold it by the cool end of the punty. Fuse the ball near the abdominal fin to the top of the candlestick shaft (photo 3), angling the fish so the ball near the back (dorsal) fin is perfectly in line with the shaft (photo 4). The fish will appear to be swimming up or down, depending on where you originally placed the attachment balls. Fuse the joint very well.

9. You can check the alignment by holding a 4 mm rod in front of the candlestick (photo 5).

10. Add the section of five balls that you made in step 4 to the

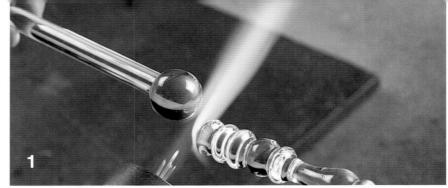

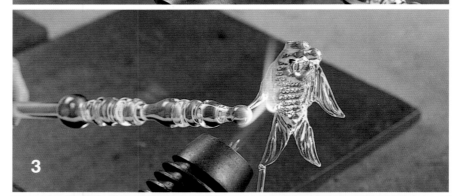

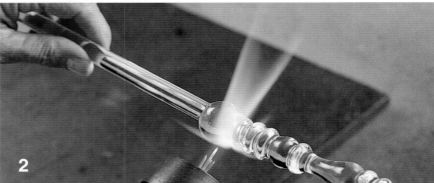

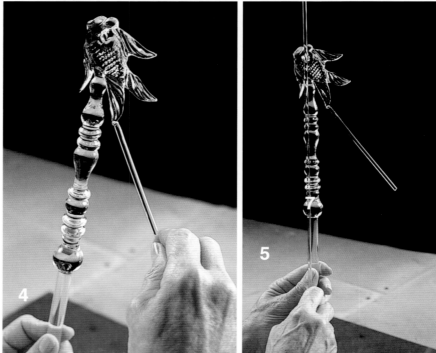

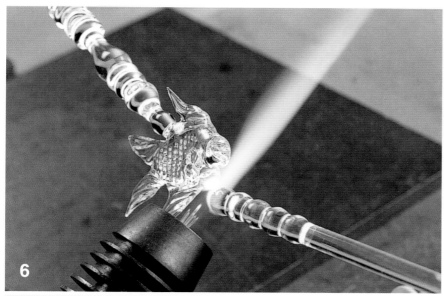

6

7

8

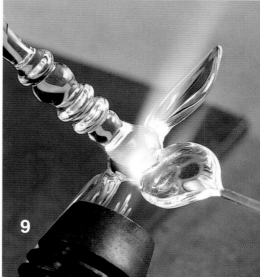

9

13. Place the candlestick in the holding kiln for 10 to 15 minutes for annealing. Leave the 12 mm turning rod attached.

14. After the candlestick has annealed, remove it from the kiln. Allow it to cool until you can comfortably hold the end with the candleholder in your ND hand.

15. Remove the 12 mm rod from the large ball. Hold each leaf by its punty, and fuse it onto the ball at about the halfway point (photos 8 and 9). Add bridges to the

attachment ball near the back (dorsal) fin of the fish, and fuse it well (photo 6). The rod attached to the section should be in line with the 12 mm turning rod. Remove the 10 mm rod from the section you've just added.

11. Make a candleholder from 25 mm tubing as described in exercise 11 on page 94. Place the candleholder in the finger tool/claw holder. Before you fuse the candleholder to the candlestick, hold it in place on top of

the section of five balls. After you look at the piece, decide whether you want to keep the length as it is. Allow your aesthetic judgment to guide you. If you want to remove some of the balls to shorten the piece, simply heat them in the flame until you can pull them off using your tweezers.

12. Heat the ball at the bottom of the candleholder, and fuse them together (photo 7).

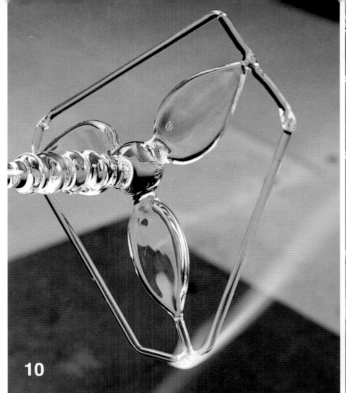

10

11

tips of the leaves to support them as you fuse them thoroughly (photos 10 and 11).

15. Remove any bridges that you've added (photos 12 and 13). Heat each leaf about ½ inch (1.3 cm) from the fuse joint, and bend it down so that the tip is below the bottom of the ball (photo 14). Line up the tips of the leaves with one another so that they balance the ball when you place it on a graphite plate (photo 15). If it doesn't stand straight, heat and bend the leaves as necessary until it does.

16. Place it in the kiln at 1050°F (566°C) to anneal.

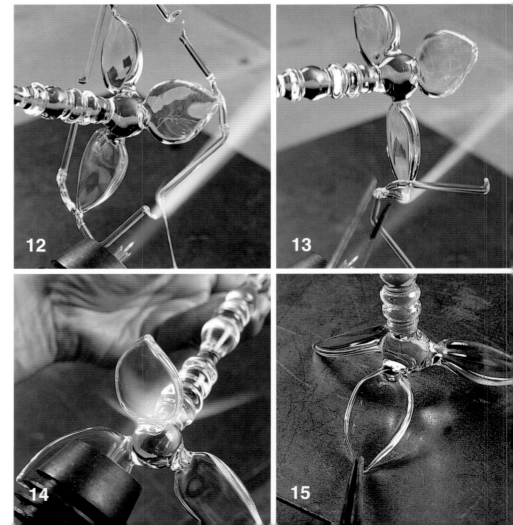

12

13

14

15

project 9—
HEART WALL SCULPTURE

In this project you'll make a heart-shaped wand that can be hung as a wall sculpture. You'll learn how to use a paper pattern as a guide for forming the glass into a heart. You can attach a plain rod or one that you've decorated with marias and transitional shapes.

materials

Clear borosilicate rods:

Several 4 mm x 6-8 inches (15.2-20.3 cm) long

3, 10 mm x 12-15 inches (30.5-38.1 cm) long

2, 12 mm x 12-15 inches (30.5-38.1 cm) long

1 ruby-colored rod, around 12 inches (30.5 cm) long

tools

Posterboard or similar heavyweight paper (optional)

Black permanent marker

Piece of chalk (optional)

Graphite plate

create half of the heart. To form the glass, heat a small section of the rod at a time, and bend it to conform to the pattern (photos 1 and 2). (Caution: If you touch paper with hot glass, it will burn.)

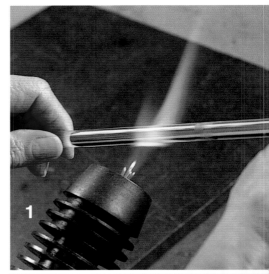

instructions

1. On a piece of posterboard, draw a heart that is about 4½ inches (11.4 cm) in length and width, or draw the pattern with chalk directly on your flameproof bench top.

2. Case a 12 mm clear rod with ruby-colored glass, fusing it well. Then pull it to a rod that is approximately 10 mm in diame-

ter. Make a series of 10 to 12 small hearts from the cased rod (see exercise 6 on page 68). (You may need to case more than one rod with color to have enough glass to make your hearts.)

3. You'll use a 10 mm clear rod and form half of the heart you drew in step 1. The rod will need to be long enough for you to hold it comfortably in each hand with enough glass left in the middle to

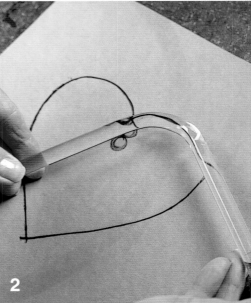

4. Hold the hot glass about 1 inch (2.5 cm) above the paper as you bend and shape it. While you bend the glass, keep the curved section in the same plane as the rod in your ND hand. (You can check this out frequently by laying the bent portion flat on your graphite plate.) If the curved portion curves away from the line, heat the rod and allow it to fall flat on the graphite plate without changing the bend.

5. When half of the heart is bent to the correct shape, use a black marker to mark off the spots where it needs to be cut later (photo 3). Remove the end of the rod at the top of the heart (photo 4).

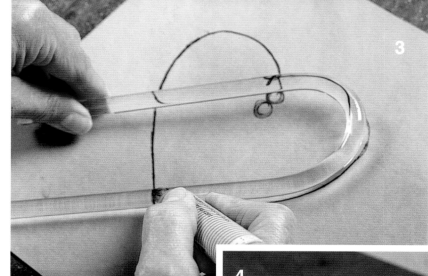

Check the alignment of the heart with the pattern (photo 5).

6. Attach a 4 mm punty to the outside of the upper curved portion of the heart (photo 6).

7. Remove the other end of the rod where you marked it, so that it conforms to your pattern.

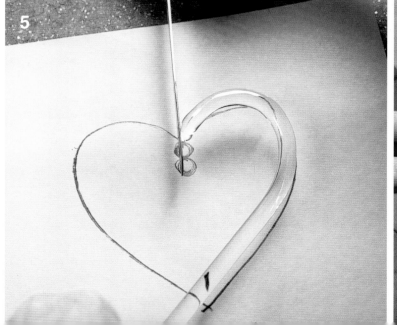

8. Repeat steps 3 through 7 to make the second half of the heart.

9. The two halves of the heart should now touch at the point in the center above and the tip below. Hold each half by its punty before heating and fusing the glass rods together where they meet at the bottom of the heart (photos 7 and 8). Then fuse the glass pieces together where they meet in the center at the top (photos 9 and 10).

10. After fusing both joints well, lay the piece flat on your graphite plate (photo 11). If the heart isn't flat, heat the glass to soften it where necessary, and try to adjust it.

11. Remove the punty in your D hand.

12. Hold the heart by the remaining punty in your ND hand, and fuse an 8- to 10-inch-long (20.3-254 cm) 10 mm rod to the tip (photo 12). Hold the heart sideways to make certain that the rod is aligned with it (photo 13). Remove the other punty.

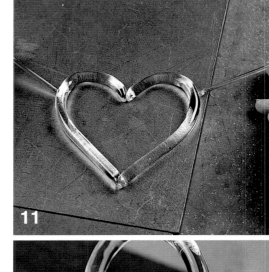

11

12

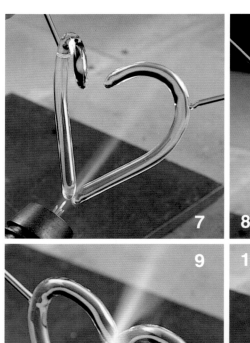

7

8

9

10

13

13. Make a loop of 4 mm glass with a punty attached. Attach the loop to one of the small red hearts (photo 14). Fuse it well.

14. Begin making a second loop from a 4 mm rod, but don't close it up. (Leave it looking like a hook.) Attach a punty to the curved portion, and fire-cut the rod so that the straight leg is about ½ inch (1.3 cm) long (photo 15).

15. Fuse the end of the straight portion of the rod just before it curves to the upper inside point of the heart (photo 16), so that the open, curved part of the loop-to-be hangs down with the opening facing you.

16. Remove the punty from the red heart with the loop. Slip the loop of the heart over the end of the hook, so that the heart hangs.

17. This is the tricky part: Heat the curved hook WITHOUT heating the heart loop, until you can bend it up so that it almost touches the straight portion (photo 17). Don't get the glass hot enough that it sticks—this time you don't want to fuse the glass together. The space only needs to be small enough that the loop on the heart doesn't slip out.

18. The red heart should dangle freely.

19. Add red hearts around the perimeter of the large clear heart, fusing each in place as you go (photos 18 and 19). (You can do this step prior to adding the dangling heart if it is easier.) Remove each punty after fusing each heart in place, and fire-polish the section from which you removed it.

20. You can make the handle of the sculpture as simple or as decorative as you like. You can leave the 10 mm rod attached as the handle, and simply finish the end, if you wish. Or, if you want to make it more decorative, remove the 10 mm rod ½ inch (1.3 cm) from the bottom of the heart, and gather a clear ball at the bottom of the heart. Create a decorated rod with a series of shapes (see exercise 4 on page 60), and attach it to the heart by the clear ball.

16

17

18

19

14

15

project 10—
FLOWER CANDLEHOLDER

*I*n this project you'll make another candleholder base similar to the one you made in project 8, but you'll assemble an entirely different looking piece with lower proportions. Through this project, you'll learn more about assembling sculptural pieces.

materials

Clear borosilicate rods:

7, 4 mm x 6-8 inches (15.2-20.3 cm) long (for punties)

2, 4 mm x 12-15 inches (30.5-38.1 cm) long (for bridges)

4, 12 mm x 12-15 inches (30.5-38.1 cm) long

Green, red, and white colored borosilicate rods

25 mm clear tubing

tools

Tweezers

Holding kiln

Finger tool/claw holder

Graphite plate

instructions

1. Case a 12 mm clear rod with a green rod, and pull it to a 12 mm rod. Make three leaves of about the same size and shape, and leave the punties attached (see exercise 3 on page 53). You might need to case more than one rod to have enough glass to make three leaves.

2. To make a flower similar to a daisy with a red center, begin by casing a clear rod in red, then create a ball at the end of it. Case a clear rod with white and make five petals with punties from the rod (see exercise 5 on page 64). Assemble the flower, fusing all of the joints well so that there are no creases anywhere, or you may have cracking later. Remove all of the punties from the flower petals except one.

3. Make a candleholder from 25 mm tubing that is about 2 inches (5.1 cm) tall (see exercise 11 on page 94).

4. Anneal all of the parts in your holding kiln set at 1050°F (566°C), placing the punties so that they protrude through the door of the kiln. (If you don't have a kiln with hole in the door, remove all of the

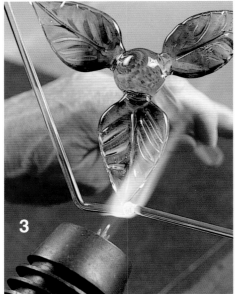

punties before placing the parts in the kiln. When you remove them, use tweezers to lift them out, and reattach the punties that you removed.) If you've used striking colors, annealing will show you in advance how the colors look together, and you'll eliminate the stress in the components before final assembly.

5. Create a large ball on the end of a 12 mm clear glass rod. Hold the rod in your ND hand away from the flame while you warm one of the leaves with your D hand at the end of the flame. While the ball is still very hot, attach a leaf to it at about the halfway point and a 90° angle to the ball (photo 1). Add the remaining two leaves, spacing them equally (photo 2). Don't bend them.

6. Attach bridges between the tips of each leaf (photo 3). (You can use the punties attached to

the tips of the leaves for this purpose, or remove them and use a 4 mm rod that is long enough to attach to all of the leaves.) Fuse the leaves to the ball well (photo 4).

7. Take the flower out of the kiln it will be very hot), and hold it by the punty.

8. Heat a spot on the top of the candleholder's ball that is centered on the turning rod. At the same time, heat the bottom of the flower using the other side of the flame (photo 5). Fuse the flower well to the top of the ball (photo 6).

9. Add some bridges from the tips of two petals down to the leaves' bridges (photo 7). Fuse the flower to the top of the ball well (photo 8).

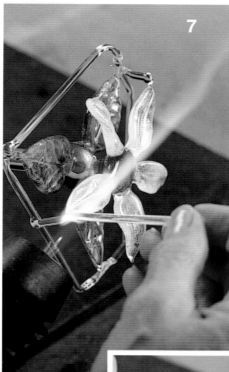

10. While all of this is still hot, place your candleholder in the claw holder, making sure that it is tightly secured (photo 9). Fuse the candleholder to the center of the flower. (Fuse both spots to a white-hot state, stick them together, count to three, and pull them apart slightly.) The holder should be straight and level. (You may have to heat and readjust until it is straight.) Remove the claw holder.

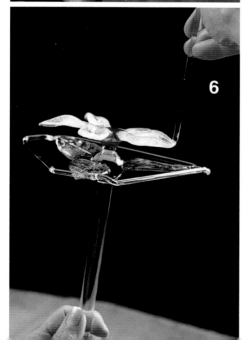

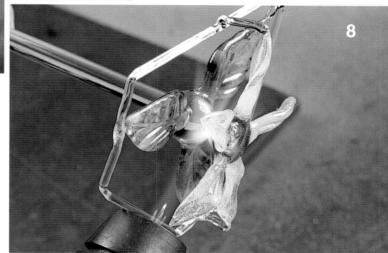

11. Remove any punties and bridges that are still attached to the piece, and clean up the areas where they were attached.

12. Place the piece in the kiln with the 12 mm rod still attached, and anneal it. Remove it from the kiln, and allow it cool just long enough that you're able to hold it by the candleholder. (Use the finger tool/claw holder, if needed.)

13. Remove the 12 mm rod (photo 10). Clean up and round off the bottom of the ball. Heat and press it on the graphite plate to flatten it slightly (photo 11).

14. Heat each leaf about ½ inch (1.3 cm) from the base until it moves easily (photo 12). Place the piece on the plate, and bend each leaf down so that it touches the plate (photo 13).

15. Rotate the candlestick around while it is sitting on the plate, and check to make sure that it's straight. If it isn't, heat and bend the necessary leaves until it is. Do this adjustment quickly, or the large ball will cool, and it may crack.

16. Place the whole piece in the kiln immediately, and soak it at the annealing temperature for approximately 15 to 30 minutes.

12

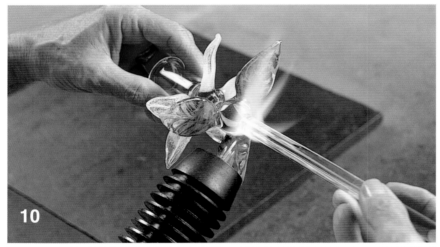

10

11

13

project 11—
FISH SCULPTURE

In this project you'll really expand your experience in making glass sculpture by using the component parts of the piece to create structural strength. You'll also be working with glass in a more improvisational way, since you'll be able to make choices as you bend and shape parts.

materials

Clear borosilicate rods:

4 mm rods (for punties and bridges)

6, 12 mm x 12-15 inches (30.5-38.1 cm) long

Colored borosilicate rods in green and other colors of your choice

tools

Holding kiln

Tweezers

Graphite plate

instructions

1. Case several 12 mm clear rods with green, and pull each rod into a 12 mm rod. To make a long, narrow leaf, create a flattened disc on the end of the cased rod (see exercise 2 on page 45). Attach a punty. Heat the disc near its base, and as it softens, begin pulling it to a width of your choice. As you work, apply the heat in front of the area that you pull. Continue this process, moving up the leaf toward the tip. Make six long leaves using this process, and leave the punties attached.

2. Make a fish using colors of your choice (see exercise 7 on page 72), and leave the punty attached.

3. Place the fish in your holding kiln with the punty sticking out the hole in the door. (If your kiln doesn't have a door, remove the punty from the fish before annealing it. Then take the hot fish out with your tweezers, and reattach the punty when you are ready to add the fish to your sculpture.)

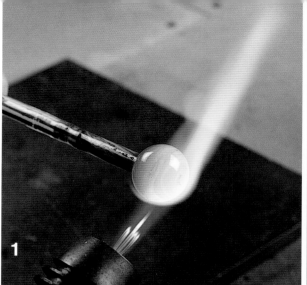

4. Case a 12 mm rod with green, and make a large ball at the end of it (photo 1). Attach three leaves to an area at the top of the ball with space between each leaf so that the bases don't touch (photo 2). Heat and bend each leaf into a natural shape as you add it (photo 3). (You could, for instance, bend it as though a current of water is flowing through it.) Remove the punties.

5. Add bridges to the tips of the leaves (photo 4), and carefully fuse the bases of the leaves one at a time so that there are no creases and all the glass flows together smoothly (photo 5).

6. Fuse the remaining three leaves to the ball, spacing them evenly around it. (These leaves will become the tripod base.) Heat and bend the leaves so that they appear to be blades of grass

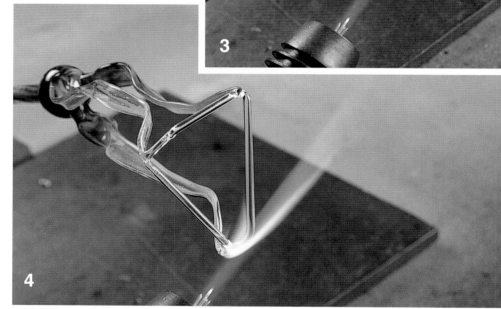

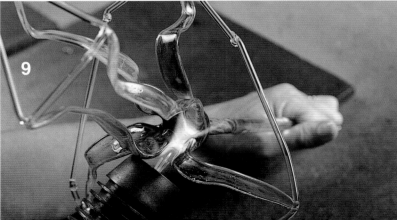

that flow up and back down again (photo 6). (Do not bend them so far down that they're in the same plane with the joint between the ball and the 12 mm rod). Remove the punties after you shape the leaves (photo 7).

7. Attach bridges to the leaves (photo 8), and fuse them really well into the ball (photos 9 and 10).

8. Remove the hot fish from the kiln, and hold it by the punty or reattach a punty. Position the fish in the grass so that the fins touch the edges of two different blades. (You might need to detach one of the blades of grass from its bridge, rebend it, and then reattach it to the bridge to have it correctly positioned. It may help to put a dot of clear glass where the joint will be. If you add the dot, fuse it well.)

9. To fuse the fish into position, attach one joint first (applying a bit of extra glass with a rod if needed) so that this joint holds the fish in place while you fuse it on the other side (photo 11). Return to the first one and

fuse it really well again. Doing this can be a bit tricky, and you should handle the glass gently.

10. Remove all the bridges and clean up the attachment points (photo 12). The fish is now a bridge between two of the leaves of grass. (This method of creating sculpture allows the parts of the sculpture to serve as structural components, giving the piece strength.)

11. Place the piece in the annealer, and allow it to soak for 15 minutes. Remove it and let it cool.

12. While the ball is still warm, remove the 12 mm rod (photo 13). Clean up the ball and round it up again (photo 14).

13. Rest the sculpture on the ball. Check to see where the lower blades of grass need to bend, so that they touch the graphite plate (photo 15). Use your tweezers to bend each one so that it becomes one of the feet for your tripod base (photo 16).

14. Anneal the whole sculpture again for 15 to 30 minutes.

15. Remove from the annealer, and allow the piece to cool.

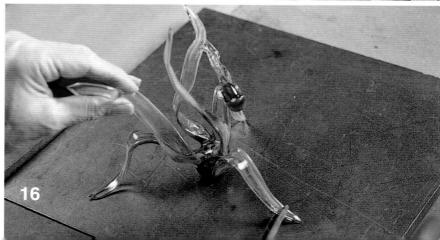

FREDERICK BIRKHILL

I'll Drink To That!, 1991
8½ x 6 x 1½ inches
(21.6 x 15.2 x 3.8 cm)
Alkyd paint, wood, flame-
worked glass
Photo by artist

FREDERICK BIRKHILL

The Visitation, 2001
11 x 4 inches
(27.9 x 10.2 cm)
Alkyd paint and flame-
worked glass
Photo by artist

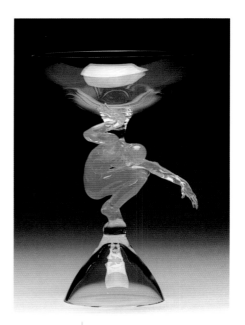

MILON TOWNSEND

Requiem, 2001
8 x 5 x 5 inches (20.3 x 12.7 x 12.7 cm)
Flameworked and coldworked glass
Photo by artist

FREDERICK BIRKHILL *Flagellate Goblet Fantasy*, 1992
6 x 12 x 7 inches (20.3 x 30.5 x 17.8 cm)
Flameworked glass
Photo by William Pelletier

MILON TOWNSEND *Deco Study #17 in Butterscotch*, 2002
20 x 12 x 8 inches (50.8 x 30.5 x 20.3 cm)
Flameworked and coldworked glass
Photo by artist

MILON TOWNSEND *Reciprocity*
11 x 6 x 6 inches (27.9 x 15.2 x 15.2 cm)
Flameworked and coldworked glass
Photo by artist

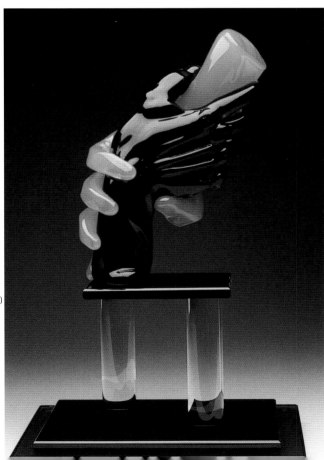

SALLY PRASCH
Splash, 2002
12 x 12 x 12 inches (30.5 x 30.5 x 30.5 cm)
Flameworked glass
Photo by Tommy Olof Elder

WARNER WHITFIELD
Flowering Cactus and Flowering Daffodil Perfume Bottles, 2002
12 x 4 x 4 inches (30.5 x 10.2 x 10.2 cm)
Blown and sculptured glass
Photo by Jonathan Wallen

WARNER WHITFIELD
Wildlife Perfume Collection, 2002
7 x 4 x 4 inches (17.8 x 10.2 x 10.2 cm)
Blown, sculptured, and sandblasted glass
Photo by Jonathan Wallen

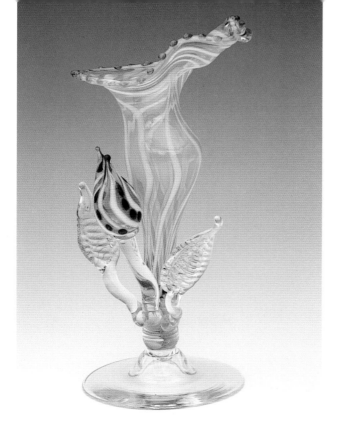

SKIP HORTON
Fleûr Vase, 2000
6 x 4 x 2½ inches (15.2 x 10.2 x 6.4 cm)
Flameworked and blown glass
Photo by Donna Beverly

VICTOR CHIARIZIA
Emergence of the Maker, 2000
14 x 6 x 6 inches (35.6 x 15.2 x 15.2 cm)
Flameworked and blown glass, hand painted
with vitreous enamels
Photo by Holly Augeri

SKIP HORTON
Florida, 2002
4 x 2½ x 2½ inches (10.2 x 6.4 x 6.4 cm)
Flameworked and blown glass
Photo by Donna Beverly

ELIZABETH RYLAND MEARS

Lollipop Series: Goblet with Twenty Lollipops, 1993.
16 x 20 x 7 inches (40.6 x 50.8 x 17.8 cm)
Flameworked, sandblasted, assembled
Photo by John Russell

BRIAN KERKVLIET

Flameworker Dude, 2001
12 inches tall (30.5 cm)
Flameworked sculpture
Photo by artist

LOY ALLEN

Phalaenopsis, 2002
16 x 9 x 7 inches (40.6 x 22.9 x 17.8 cm)
Welded steel and flameworked glass
Photo by Sid Spelts

BRIAN KERKVLIET | *Offering to the Sea Critters*, 1998
16 inches tall (40.6 cm)
Flameworked sculpture with furnace-
blown offering bowl
Photo by artist

BRIAN KERKVLIET | *Italian Style Optic Goblet Group*, 2000
8-12 inches tall (20.3 to 30.5 cm)
Flameworked goblets
Photo by artist

LOY ALLEN | *Floral Goblets*, 2002
13 x 4 x 4 inches (33 x 10.2 x 10.2 cm)
Flameworked glass
Photo by Sid Spelts

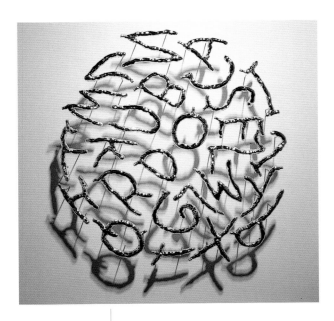

JILL REYNOLDS *Beauty*, 2000
27 x 26 x 5 inches (68.6 x 66 x 12.7 cm)
Blown glass, mirrored
Photo by Arthur Aubry

JILL REYNOLDS *Beauty* (detail), 2000
Photo by Arthur Aubry

JILL REYNOLDS

Alphabet, 1997
10½ x 34 x 3 inches (26.7 x 86.4 x 7.6 cm)
Curved wall installation pierced by 11,000 blown
glass bubbles blown on site over period of seven
weeks; backlit with fluorescent lights
Photo by Charles Mayer

JILL REYNOLDS

Alphabet (detail), 1997
Photo by Charles Mayer

MARCO JERMEN *Night Sky Marble*, 2000
1½ x 1½ inches (3.8 x 3.8 cm)
Flameworked glass
Photo by Jim King

KAREN BUHLER *Golden Seedpod Sconce*, 2001
18 x 12 x 6 inches (45.7 x 30.5 x 15.2 cm)
Flameworked rod, sandblasted, lustered, and
wall mounted
Photo by artist

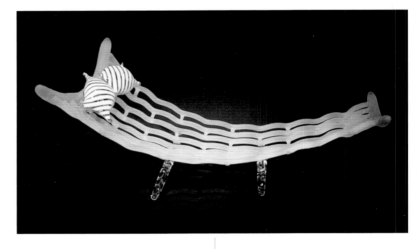

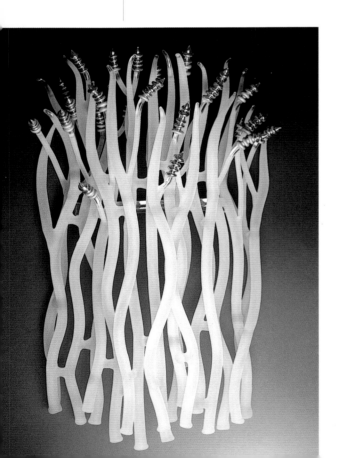

KAREN BUHLER *Vacation For Two*, 1999
7 x 19 x 12 inches (17.8 x 48.3 x 30.5 cm)
Lampworked and kiln-formed rod with tube
blown pillows, sandblasted
Photo by artist

TIM JERMAN
Hermit Crab with Anemones, 2000
6 x 5 x 6 inches (15.2 x 12.7 x 15.2 cm)
Flameworked colored glass and natural shell
Photo by Jerry Anthony

TIM JERMAN
Nautilus, 2001
4 x 5 x 2 inches (10.2 x 12.7 x 5 cm)
Flameworked colored glass and natural shell
Photo by Jerry Anthony

**JAMES
MINSON**
Octopus Chandelier, 2001
24 x 34 x 24 inches (61 x 86.4 x 61 cm)
Glass with electric lights
Photo by artist

EMILIO SANTINI

Miniature Incalmo Bottles, 1998
1 x 1 x ½ to 1 x 1 x 2½ inches (2.5 x 2.5 x 1.3 to 2.5 x 2.5 x 6.4 cm)
Blown glass
Photo by Julian Withers-Dixon

EMILIO SANTINI

Venus and Adonis, 1998
4 x 4 x 19 inches (10.2 x 10.2 x 48.3 cm)
Blown and sculpted glass
Photo by Julian Withers-Dixon

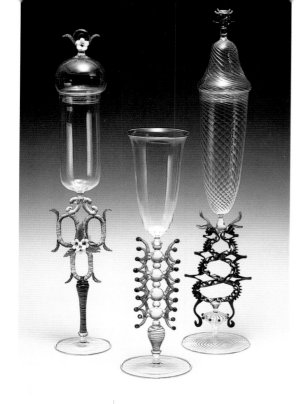

ROGER PARRAMORE

Four Cups, 2001
Tallest cup: 24 inches (61 cm)
Flameworked glass
Photo by artist

EMILIO SANTINI

Vessels with Lids, 1998
4 x 4 x 18 to 5 x 5 x 26 inches
(10.2 x 10.2 x 45.7 to 12.7 x
12.7 x 66 cm)
Blown and sculpted glass
Photo by Julian Withers-Dixon

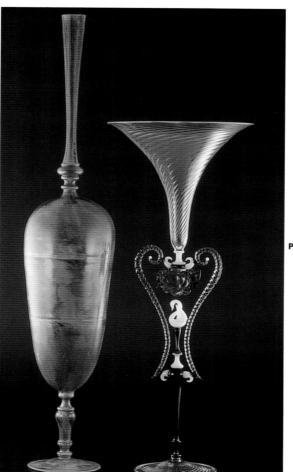

**ROGER
PARRAMORE**

Swan Cup and Vessel, 2001
Vessel: 30 x 5 inches (76.2 x 12.7 cm);
cup: 24 x 8 inches (61 x 20.3 cm)
Flameworked glass
Photo by artist

JAMES MINSON *Polyps*, 2002
8 x 24 x 6 inches each (20.3 x 61 x 15.2 cm)
Glass and wood
Photo by artist

BANDHU SCOTT DUNHAM *Sphere Grouping*, 1998
11 x 20 x 14 inches (27.9 x 50.8 x 35.6 cm)
Flameworked glass, slumped
Photo by Marchetti

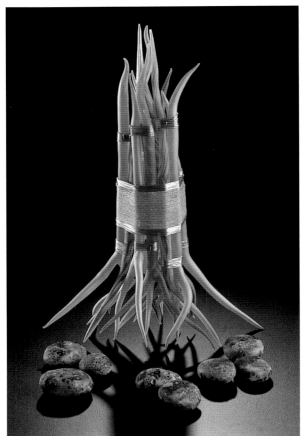

ELIZABETH RYLAND MEARS *Small Bundle of Twigs with Stones*, 2001
10 x 6 x 4 inches (25.4 x 15.2 x 10.2 cm)
Flameworked glass with sandblasted lusters,
copper, and waxed linen
Photo by Tommy Olof Elder

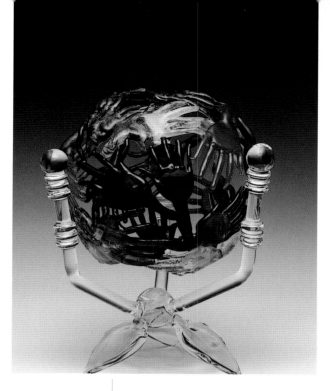

ELIZABETH RYLAND MEARS

Hand Ball Anyone? - Closed Form Series, 1994
11 x 9 x 9 inches (27.9 x 22.9 x 22.9 cm)
Flameworked glass
Photo by John Russell

ELIZABETH RYLAND MEARS

Bowl Series: Aqua Iridized with Leaf Motif, 1994.
3½ x 8 x 8 inches (8.9 x 20.3 x 20.3 cm)
Flat glass; fused, slumped, sandblasted, glass,
flameworked, assembled
Photo by John Russell

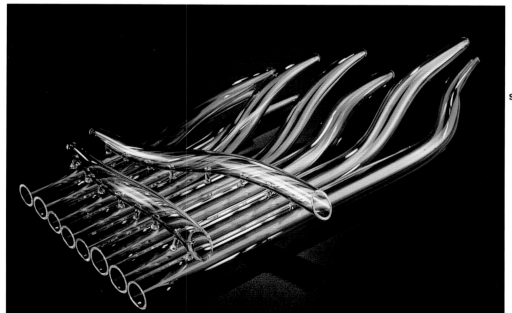

SALLY PRASCH

Pan Pipes, 1997
9 x 3/4 x 5 inches (22.9 x 1.9 x 12.7 cm)
Flameworked glass
Photo by Tommy Olof Elder

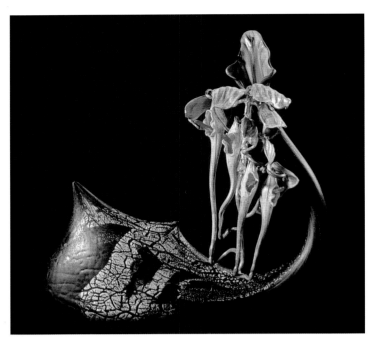

VICTOR CHIARIZIA

Gaia in the Night Sky, 2001
13 x 12 x 4 inches (33 x 30.5 x 10.2 cm)
Flameworked and blown glass, hand
painted with vitreous enamels
Photo by Holly Augeri

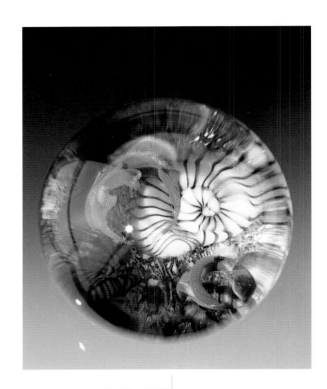

MARCO JERMAN

Under Sea Marble, 2000
1⅝ x 1⅝ inches (4.1 x 4.1 cm)
Flameworked handmade murrinis
on dichroic glass
Photo by Jerry Anthony

VICTOR CHIARIZIA

Hidden Desires, 2002
20 x 8 x 8 inches (50.8 x 20.3 x 20.3 cm)
Flameworked and blown glass, hand painted
with vitreous enamels
Photo by Holly Augeri

MARGARET NEHER

Cypripedium Cordigerum, . 2002
9 x 6 x 5½ inches (22.9 x 15.2 x 14 cm)
Flameworked glass
Photo by Dan Neuberger

MARK PAYTON

Transformation Piece, 2002
27 x 15 x 12 inches (68.6 x 38.1 x 30.5 cm)
Freehand sculptured glass
Photo by Geoffrey Carr

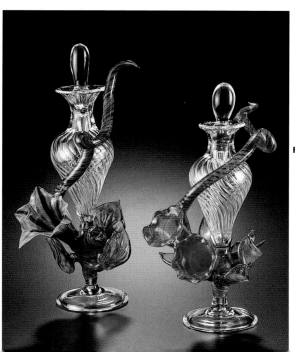

**ELIZABETH
RYLAND MEARS**

*Stoppered Bottles with Morning Glory
and Trumpet Vine*, 2002
9 x 5 x 4 inches (22.9 x 12.7 x 10.2 cm)
Flameworked and blown glass
Photo by Tommy Olof Elder

BRIAN KERKVLEIT

Awakening of the Swamp Consciousness, 1993
15 inches (38.1 cm) tall
Furnace blown glass with flameworked imagery
Photo by artist

**ELIZABETH RYLAND MEARS
AND L. LINDSEY MEARS**

Accordion Book: The NAGA Book, 2001
12 x 18 x 6 inches (30.5 x 45.7 x 15.2 cm)
Flameworked and sandblasted glass; photos
Photo by Tommy Olof Elder

SALLY PRASCH

Thinking of Fish Jumping, 1990
10 x 8 x 6 inches (25.4 x 20.3 x 15.2 cm)
Flameworked glass
Photo by Tommy Olof Elder

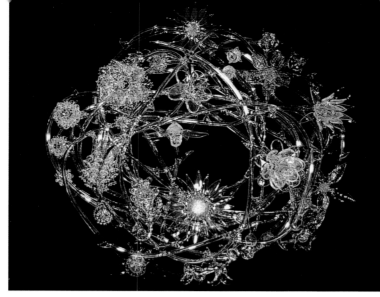

JAMES MINSON | *Wreath*, 2000
20 x 8 inches (50.8 x 20.3 cm)
Flameworked glass
Photo by artist

MILON TOWNSEND

Acropolis, 2002
12 x 16 x 5 inches (30.5 x 40.6 x 12.7 cm)
Flameworked and coldworked glass
Photo by artist

KAREN BUHLER | *Rain Changing to Showers*, 2002
23 x 10 x 4½ (58.4 x 25.4 x 11.4 cm)
Flameworked tube; sandblasted, lustered, wallmounted
Photo by artist

glossary

Annealing: Heating glass to a certain temperature in the kiln or in the flame of the torch to relieve internal stress.

Borosilicate glass: Glass containing borax as flux that was originally formulated for making scientific equipment. (It is also called "hard glass".) This kind of glass has a low coefficient of expansion.

Bridge system: A system built from small rods to support glass parts during fusing.

Coefficient of expansion: The measurement of how much a material expands or contracts at a fixed range of temperature.

Compatibility: The measure of whether glass can be combined with other types of glass (or other materials) in the molten state and survive the cooling process without cracking.

Creases: Sharp indentations in the surface of the glass, usually formed where two pieces of glass are joined.

Devitrification: The anomalous formation of crystals on the surface of the glass that make the glass appear frosted.

Fire-cut: Using the torch to "cut" the stringer on a glass rod.

Fire-polishing: Reheating the surface of the glass to remove imperfections.

Flashback arrestor: A device that allows gas to flow in only one direction. These can be attached to both oxygen and propane tanks to prevent ingnited gases from flowing backwards into the tank.

Frit: Crushed colored glass that comes in various grit sizes. Finely ground frit is powder. (Always wear a mask when using frit.)

Fulgurite: A form of natural glass, usually tube-shaped, that is formed whenlightning strikes sand.

Gather: A mass of molten glass.

Hard glass: Another term for borosilicate glass.

Heat differential: The difference in temperature between two adjacent areas of glass.

Heat shock: Changing the temperature of glass too quickly.

Internal mix torch: A torch in which gases are mixed together within the body before emerging at the surface.

Neutral flame: A torch flame in which the gases are equally mixed.

Obsidian: Natural glass created by volcanic activity.

Oxidation/reduction colors: Borosilicate glass rods in which the colors are affected by the atmosphere of the flame used when working with them.

Oxides: Molecules that have some other element combined with oxygen. In flameworking, oxides of metals are used to create color in clear glass.

Oxidizing flame: A flame that is high in oxygen content.

Points: Long, tapered sections of glass pulled from glass tubing.

Polariscope: An instrument that shows the stress patterns in glass.

Pulling points: Drawing out the end of a glass tube to make a handle and a blowpipe.

Punty: A temporary handle attached to a glass object to facilitate working with it in the flame.

Reducing flame: A flame that is high in propane.

Soaking: Leaving glass in the kiln at a given temperature for a particular period of time. When annealing glass, this process releases stresses within the glass.

Soft glass: A term used to describe glass containing lead or soda-lime as flux that has a much higher coefficient of expansion than hard glass.

Striking colors: Colored glass that is clear when molten and colored after annealing.

Surface mix torch: a torch which brings the gases to the surface where they are mixed as they emerge.

acknowledgments

Thanks...

To all the artists who so generously contributed photographs for this book.

To Michael Mears who continues to be an invaluable source of information, advice, and support. I rely heavily on his engineering expertise, and, with his encouragement, have developed the technical skills necessary to create the pieces that I envision. He is a constant source of help.

To the following teachers and mentors who have shared knowledge, techniques, and have provided a sense of the community and history of glassmakers: Loy Allen, Fred Birkhill, Ellie Burke, Einar and Jamex de la Torre, Bandhu Scott Dunham, Shane Fero, Suellen Fowler, Dinah Hulet, Tim Jerman, Brian Kerkvliet, Robert Mickelsen, James Minson, Margaret Neher, Don Niblack, Roger Parramore, Susan Plum, Sally Prasch, Jill Reynolds, Emilio Santini, Hubert Stern, Milon Townsend, and Warner Whitfield.

To my photographer, Tommy Olof Elder, who continues to make insightful images of my creations.

To Karen King, Nichole O'Neill, and Robert Ryland who read the first drafts of this book and offered valuable changes and/or additions.

To Carol Taylor at Lark Books, who first challenged me to write this book.

To my editor, Katherine Aimone, the purveyor of puns, who kept me on track throughout the entire process and has edited my drafts in a sterling manner. Through the intelligence, good humor, dry wit, and hard work of my team at Lark Books, this book has come into fruition.

To photographers Keith and Wendy Wright, for their expertise that provided the necessary visual components of this book for the beginning glassmaker. Their good humor made photo sessions fun.

To art director Tom Metcalf, who expertly fashioned the layout of this book. His commitment to make the book both beautiful and informative is evident throughout.

Lastly, to all of my students who continue to come to me for instruction and teach me so much in return.

about the author

Elizabeth Ryland Mears is a full-time studio artist who creates works in glass and mixed media.

She began flameworking in the early 1990s after working in flat glass techniques and teaching at such places as the Smithsonian Institution and the Building Museum in Washington, D.C. After discovering her love for flameworking, she studied at Penland School of Crafts in Penland, North Carolina; Pilchuck Glass School in Stanwood, Washington (where she was a scholarship student); and the Studio of the Corning Museum of Glass in Corning, New York (also as a scholarship student). She was a teaching assistant at Pilchuck during 2001, and now teaches her own classes at Penland.

She creates sculptural as well as limited production pieces. The sculpture combines flameworked glass with mixed media in wall and pedestal pieces. Her production pieces include goblets, candlesticks, bottles, and other items. Whether representational or conceptual, all of her work reflects a strong connection with nature and cyclical time. Both bodies of work are presented by galleries throughout the United States and Canada and are included in many private collections.

In the juried exhibit, *North American Glass 2002*, she received an award of second place for a piece entitled *Standing Book: The Bone Woman Unfurling* that she created in collaboration with her daughter Lindsey Mears. Her work was selected by the Kentucky Arts and Crafts Foundation for exhibit in *Southern Women of Influence* and was also exhibited by the Hsinchu Museum of Taiwan in 2001. Her *Botanical Series* goblets and bottles were exhibited at the Botanical Museum of the Harvard Museum of Natural History in the summer of 2002, as well as at the *20th Anniversary Benefit Celebrating Craft* at the Renwick Gallery in Washington, D.C. Her glass creations have been included in numerous other group exhibitions exploring flameworked glass.

index